DON CARLOS

A PLAY

FRIEDRICH SCHILLER

ACT I.

SCENE I.

The Royal Gardens in Aranjuez. CARLOS and DOMINGO.

DOMINGO.

Our pleasant sojourn in Aranjuez

Is over now, and yet your highness quits These joyous scenes no happier than before. Our visit hath been fruitless. Oh, my prince, Break this mysterious and gloomy silence! Open your heart to your own father's heart! A monarch never can too dearly buy

The peace of his own son--his only son.

[CARLOS looks on the ground in silence.

Is there one dearest wish that bounteous Heaven Hath e'er withheld from her most favored child? I stood beside, when in Toledo's walls

The lofty Charles received his vassals' homage, When conquered princes thronged to kiss his hand, And there at once six mighty kingdoms fell

In fealty at his feet: I stood and marked

The young, proud blood mount to his glowing cheek, I saw his bosom swell with high resolves, His eye, all radiant with triumphant pride, Flash through the assembled throng; and that same eye Confessed, "Now am I wholly satisfied!"

[CARLOS turns away.

This silent sorrow, which for eight long moons Hath hung its shadows, prince, upon your brow-- The mystery of the court, the nation's grief-- Hath cost your father many a sleepless night, And many a tear of anguish to your mother.

CARLOS (turning hastily round).

My mother! Grant, O heaven, I may forget How she became my mother!

DOMINGO.

Gracious prince!

CARLOS (passing his hands thoughtfully over his brow). Alas! alas! a fruitful source of woe Have mothers been to me. My youngest act, When first these eyes beheld the light of day, Destroyed a mother.

DOMINGO.

Is it possible That this reproach disturbs your conscience, prince?

CARLOS.

And my new mother! Hath she not already Cost me my father's heart? Scarce loved at best. My claim to some small favor lay in this-- I was his only child! 'Tis over! She Hath blest him with a daughter--and who knows What slumbering ills the future hath in store?

DOMINGO.

You jest, my prince. All Spain adores its queen. Shall it be thought that you, of all the world, Alone should view her with the eyes of hate-- Gaze on her charms, and yet be coldly wise?

How, prince? The loveliest lady of her time, A queen withal, and once your own betrothed? No, no, impossible--it cannot be!

Where all men love, you surely cannot hate. Carlos could never so belie himself.

I prithee, prince, take heed she do not learn That she hath lost her son's regard. The news Would pain her deeply.

CARLOS. Ay, sir! think you so?

DOMINGO.

Your highness doubtless will remember how, At the late tournament in Saragossa, A lance's splinter struck our gracious sire. The queen, attended by her ladies, sat High in the centre gallery of the palace, And looked upon the fight. A cry arose, "The king! he bleeds!" Soon through the general din, A rising murmur strikes upon her ear.

"The prince--the prince!" she cries, and forward rushed, As though to leap down from the balcony, When a voice answered, "No, the king himself!" "Then send for his physicians!" she replied, And straight regained her former self-composure.

[After a short pause.

But you seem wrapped in thought?

CARLOS. In wonder, sir, That the king's merry confessor should own So rare a skill in the romancer's art.

[Austerely.

Yet have I heard it said that those Who watch men's looks and carry tales about, Have done more mischief in this world of ours Than the assassin's knife, or poisoned bowl.

Your labor, Sir, hath been but ill-bestowed; Would you win thanks, go seek them of the king.

DOMINGO.

This caution, prince, is wise. Be circumspect With men--but not with every man alike.

Repel not friends and hypocrites together; I mean you well, believe me!

CARLOS. Say you so?

Let not my father mark it, then, or else Farewell your hopes forever of the purple.

DOMINGO (starts).

CARLOS.

How!

CARLOS. Even so! Hath he not promised you The earliest purple in the gift of Spain?

DOMINGO.

You mock me, prince!

CARLOS. Nay! Heaven forefend, that I Should mock that awful man whose fateful lips Can doom my father or to heaven or hell!

DOMINGO.

I dare not, prince, presume to penetrate The sacred mystery of your secret grief, Yet I implore your highness to remember

That, for a conscience ill at ease, the church Hath opened an asylum, of which kings

Hold not the key--where even crimes are purged Beneath the holy sacramental seal.

You know my meaning, prince--I've said enough.

CARLOS.

No! be it, never said, I tempted so The keeper of that seal.

DOMINGO.

Prince, this mistrust-- You wrong the most devoted of your servants.

CARLOS.

Then give me up at once without a thought Thou art a holy man--the world knows that-- But, to speak plain, too zealous far for me. The road to Peter's chair is long and rough, And too much knowledge might encumber you. Go, tell this to the king, who sent thee hither!

DOMINGO.

Who sent me hither?

CARLOS. Ay! Those were my words.

Too well-too well, I know, that I'm betrayed, Slandered on every hand--that at this court A hundred eyes are hired to watch my steps. I know, that royal Philip to his slaves Hath sold his only son, and every wretch, Who takes account of each half-uttered word, Receives such princely guerdon as was ne'er Bestowed on deeds of honor, Oh, I know But hush!--no more of that! My heart will else O'erflow and I've already said too much.

DOMINGO.

The king is minded, ere the set of sun, To reach Madrid: I see the court is mustering. Have I permission, prince?

CARLOS. I'll follow straight.

[Exit DOMINGO.

CARLOS (after a short silence).

O wretched Philip! wretched as thy son! Soon shall thy bosom bleed at every pore, Torn by suspicion's poisonous serpent fang. Thy fell sagacity full soon shall pierce The fatal secret it is bent to know, And thou wilt madden, when it breaks upon thee!

SCENE II.

CARLOS, MARQUIS OF POSA. CARLOS.

Lo! Who comes here? 'Tis he! O ye kind heavens, My Roderigo!

MARQUIS. Carlos! CARLOS. Can it be?

And is it truly thou? O yes, it is!

I press thee to my bosom, and I feel

Thy throbbing heart beat wildly 'gainst mine own. And now all's well again. In this embrace My sick, sad heart is comforted. I hang Upon my Roderigo's neck!

MARQUIS. Thy heart!

Thy sick sad heart! And what is well again What needeth to be well? Thy words amaze me.

CARLOS.

What brings thee back so suddenly from Brussels? Whom must I thank for this most glad surprise?

And dare I ask? Whom should I thank but thee, Thou gracious and all bounteous Providence?

Forgive me, heaven! if joy hath crazed my brain.

Thou knewest no angel watched at Carlos' side, And sent me this! And yet I ask who sent him.

MARQUIS.

Pardon, dear prince, if I can only meet With wonder these tumultuous ecstacies. Not thus I looked to find Don Philip's son. A hectic red burns on your pallid cheek, And your lips quiver with a feverish heat.

What must I think, dear prince? No more I see The youth of lion heart, to whom I come The envoy of a brave and suffering people. For now I stand not here as Roderigo-- Not as the playmate of the stripling Carlos-- But, as the deputy of all mankind, I clasp thee thus:--'tis Flanders that clings here Around thy neck, appealing with my tears To thee for succor in her bitter need. This land is lost, this land so dear to thee, If Alva, bigotry's relentless tool, Advance on Brussels with his Spanish laws. This noble country's last faint hope depends On thee, loved scion of imperial Charles!

And, should thy noble heart forget to beat In human nature's cause, Flanders is lost!

CARLOS.

Then it is lost.

MARQUIS.

What do I hear? Alas!

CARLOS.

Thou speakest of times that long have passed away. I, too, have had my visions of a Carlos, Whose cheek would fire at freedom's glorious name, But he, alas! has long been in his grave. He, thou seest here, no longer is that Carlos, Who took his leave of thee in Alcala, Who in the fervor of a youthful heart, Resolved, at some no distant time, to wake The golden age in Spain! Oh, the conceit, Though but a child's, was yet divinely fair! Those dreams are past!

MARQUIS.

Said you, those dreams, my prince! And were they only dreams?

CARLOS.

Oh, let me weep, Upon thy bosom weep these burning tears, My only friend! Not one have I--not one-- In the wide circuit of this earth,--not one Far as the sceptre of my sire extends,

Far as the navies bear the flag of Spain, There is no spot--none--none, where I dare yield An outlet to my tears, save only this.

I charge thee, Roderigo! Oh, by all The hopes we both do entertain of heaven, Cast me not off from thee, my friend, my friend!

[POSA bends over him in silent emotion. Look on me, Posa, as an orphan child, Found near the throne, and nurtured by thy love. Indeed, I know not what a father is. I am a monarch's son. Oh, were it so, As my heart tells me that it surely is, That thou from millions hast been chosen out To comprehend my being; if it be true, That all-creating nature has designed In me to reproduce a Roderigo, And on the morning of our life attuned Our souls' soft concords to the selfsame key; If one poor tear, which gives my heart relief, To thee were dearer than my father's favor----

MARQUIS.

Oh, it is dearer far than all the world!

CARLOS.

I'm fallen so low, have grown so poor withal, I must recall to thee our childhood's years,-- Must ask thee payment of a debt incurred When thou and I were scarce to boyhood grown. Dost thou remember, how we grew together, Two daring youths, like brothers, side by side?

I had no sorrow but to see myself Eclipsed by thy bright genius. So I vowed, Since I might never cope with thee in power, That I would love thee with excess of love.

Then with a thousand shows of tenderness, And warm affection, I besieged thy heart, Which cold and proudly still repulsed them all. Oft have I stood, and--yet thou sawest it never Hot bitter tear-drops brimming in mine eyes, When I have marked thee, passing me unheeded, Fold to thy bosom youths of humbler birth. "Why only these?" in anguish, once I asked-- "Am I not kind and good to thee as they?"

But dropping on thy knees, thine answer came, With an unloving look of cold reserve, "This is my duty to the monarch's son!"

MARQUIS.

Oh, spare me, dearest prince, nor now recall Those boyish acts that make me blush for shame.

CARLOS.

I did not merit such disdain from thee-- You might despise me, crush my heart, but never Alter my love. Three times didst thou repulse The prince, and thrice he came to thee again, To beg thy love, and force on thee his own.

At length chance wrought what Carlos never could. Once we were playing, when thy shuttlecock Glanced off and struck my aunt, Bohemia's queen, Full in the face! She thought 'twas with intent, And all in tears complained unto the king. The palace youth were summoned on the spot, And charged to name the culprit. High in wrath The king vowed vengeance for the deed: "Although It were his son, yet still should he be made A dread example!" I looked around and marked Thee stand aloof, all trembling with dismay.

Straight I stepped forth; before the royal feet I flung myself, and cried, "'Twas I who did it; Now let thine anger fall upon thy son!"

MARQUIS.

Ah, wherefore, prince, remind me?

CARLOS.

Hear me further!

Before the face of the assembled court, That stood, all pale with pity, round about, Thy Carlos was tied up, whipped like a slave; I looked on thee, and wept not. Blow rained on blow; I gnashed my teeth with pain, yet wept I not!

My royal blood streamed 'neath the pitiless lash; I looked on thee, and wept not. Then you came, And fell half-choked with sobs before my feet: "Carlos," you cried, "my pride is overcome; I will repay thee when thou art a king."

MARQUIS (stretching forth his hand to CARLOS). Carlos, I'll keep my word; my boyhood's vow I now as man renew. I will repay thee.

Some day, perchance, the hour may come----

CARLOS.

Now! now!

The hour has come; thou canst repay me all. I have sore need of love. A fearful secret Burns in my breast; it must--it must be told. In thy pale looks my death-doom will I read. Listen; be petrified; but answer not.

I love--I love--my mother!

MARQUIS.

O my God!

CARLOS.

Nay, no forbearance! spare me not! Speak! speak! Proclaim aloud, that on this earth's great round There is no misery to compare with mine.

Speak! speak!--I know all--all that thou canst say The son doth love his mother. All the world's Established usages, the course of nature,

Rome's fearful laws denounce my fatal passion. My suit conflicts with my own father's rights, I feel it all, and yet I love. This path Leads on to madness, or the scaffold. I Love without hope, love guiltily, love madly, With anguish, and with peril of my life; I see, I see it all, and yet I love.

MARQUIS.

The queen--does she know of your passion?

CARLOS.

Could I

Reveal it to her? She is Philip's wife-- She is the queen, and this is Spanish ground, Watched by a jealous father, hemmed around By ceremonial forms, how, how could I Approach her unobserved? 'Tis now eight months, Eight maddening months, since the king summoned me Home from my studies, since I have been doomed To look on her, adore her day by day, And all the while be silent as the grave!

Eight maddening months, Roderigo; think of this! This fire has seethed and raged within my breast! A thousand, thousand times, the dread confession Has mounted to my lips, yet evermore Shrunk, like a craven, back upon my heart. O Roderigo! for a few brief moments Alone with her!

MARQUIS.

Ah! and your father, prince!

CARLOS.

Unhappy me! Remind me not of him.

Tell me of all the torturing pangs of conscience, But speak not, I implore you, of my father!

MARQUIS.

Then do you hate your father?

CARLOS.

No, oh, no!

I do not hate my father; but the fear That guilty creatures feel,--a shuddering dread,-- Comes o'er me ever at that terrible name.

Am I to blame, if slavish nurture crushed Love's tender germ within my youthful heart? Six years I'd numbered, ere the fearful man, They told me was my father, met mine eyes.

One morning 'twas, when with a stroke I saw him Sign four death-warrants. After that I ne'er Beheld him, save when, for some childish fault, I was brought out for chastisement. O God! I feel my heart grow bitter at the thought.

Let us away! away!

MARQUIS.

Nay, Carlos, nay, You must, you shall give all your sorrow vent, Let it have words! 'twill ease your o'erfraught heart.

CARLOS.

Oft have I struggled with myself, and oft At midnight, when my guards were sunk in sleep, With floods of burning tears I've sunk before The image of the ever-blessed Virgin, And craved a filial heart, but all in vain. I rose with prayer unheard. O Roderigo!

Unfold this wondrous mystery of heaven, Why of a thousand fathers only this Should fall to me--and why to him this son, Of many thousand better? Nature could not In her wide orb have found two opposites More diverse in their elements. How could She bind the two extremes of human kind-- Myself and him--in one so holy bond?

O dreadful fate! Why was it so decreed? Why should two men, in all things else apart, Concur so fearfully in one desire?

Roderigo, here thou seest two hostile stars, That in the lapse of ages, only once, As they sweep onwards in their orbed course, Touch with a crash that shakes them to the centre, Then rush apart forever and forever.

MARQUIS.

I feel a dire foreboding.

CARLOS.

So do I. Like hell's grim furies, dreams of dreadful shape Pursue me still. My better genius strives With the fell projects of a dark despair.

My wildered subtle spirit crawls through maze On maze of sophistries, until at length It gains a yawning precipice's brink. O Roderigo! should I e'er in him Forget the father--ah! thy deathlike look Tells me I'm understood--should I forget The father--what were then the king to me?

MARQUIS (after a pause).

One thing, my Carlos, let me beg of you!

Whate'er may be your plans, do nothing,--nothing,-- Without your friend's advice. You promise this?

CARLOS.

All, all I promise that thy love can ask! I throw myself entirely upon thee!

MARQUIS.

The king, I hear, is going to Madrid.

The time is short. If with the queen you would Converse in private, it is only here, Here in Aranjuez, it can be done.

The quiet of the place, the freer manners, All favor you.

CARLOS.

And such, too, was my hope; But it, alas! was vain.

MARQUIS.

Not wholly so.

I go to wait upon her. If she be The same in Spain she was in Henry's court, She will be frank at least. And if I can Read any hope for Carlos in her looks-- Find her inclined to grant an interview-- Get her attendant ladies sent away----

CARLOS.

Most of them are my friends—especially The Countess Mondecar, whom I have gained By service to her son, my page.

MARQUIS.

'Tis well; Be you at hand, and ready to appear, Whene'er I give the signal, prince.

CARLOS.

I will,-- Be sure I will:--and all good speed attend thee!

MARQUIS.

I will not lose a moment; so, farewell. [Exeunt severally.

SCENE III.

The Queen's Residence in Aranjuez. The Pleasure Grounds, intersected by an avenue, terminated by the Queen's Palace.

The QUEEN, DUCHESS OF OLIVAREZ, PRINCESS OF EBOLI, and MARCHIONESS OF MONDECAR, all advancing from the avenue.

QUEEN (to the MARCHIONESS).

I will have you beside me, Mondecar.

The princess, with these merry eyes of hers, Has plagued me all the morning. See, she scarce Can hide the joy she feels to leave the country.

EBOLI.

'Twere idle to conceal, my queen, that I Shall be most glad to see Madrid once more.

MONDECAR.

And will your majesty not be so, too? Are you so grieved to quit Aranjuez?

QUEEN.

To quit--this lovely spot at least I am.

This is my world. Its sweetness oft and oft Has twined itself around my inmost heart. Here, nature, simple, rustic nature greets me, The sweet companion of my early years-- Here I indulge once more my childhood's sports, And my dear France's gales come blowing here. Blame not this partial fondness--all hearts yearn For their own native land.

EBOLI.

But then how lone, How dull and lifeless it is here! We might As well be in La Trappe.

QUEEN.

I cannot see it.

To me Madrid alone is lifeless. But What saith our duchess to it?

OLIVAREZ.

Why, methinks, Your majesty, since kings have ruled in Spain, It hath been still the custom for the court To pass the summer months alternately Here and at Pardo,--in Madrid, the winter.

QUEEN.

Well, I suppose it has! Duchess, you know I've long resigned all argument with you.

MONDECAR.

Next month Madrid will be all life and bustle. They're fitting up the Plaza Mayor now,

And we shall have rare bull-fights; and, besides, A grand auto da fe is promised us.

QUEEN.

Promised? This from my gentle Mondecar!

MONDECAR.

Why not? 'Tis only heretics they burn!

QUEEN.

I hope my Eboli thinks otherwise!

EBOLI.

What, I? I beg your majesty may think me As good a Christian as the marchioness.

QUEEN.

Alas! I had forgotten where I am,--

No more of this! We were speaking, I think, About the country? And methinks this month Has flown away with strange rapidity.

I counted on much pleasure, very much, From our retirement here, and yet I have not Found that which I expected. Is it thus With all our hopes? And yet I cannot say One wish of mine is left ungratified.

OLIVAREZ.

You have not told us, Princess Eboli, If there be hope for Gomez,--and if we may Expect ere long to greet you as his bride?

QUEEN.

True--thank you, duchess, for reminding me!

[Addressing the PRINCESS.

I have been asked to urge his suit with you. But can I do it? The man whom I reward With my sweet Eboli must be a man Of noble stamp indeed.

OLIVAREZ.

And such he is, A man of mark and fairest fame,--a man Whom our dear monarch signally has graced With his most royal favor.

QUEEN.

He's happy in Such high good fortune; but we fain would know, If he can love, and win return of love.

This Eboli must answer.

EBOLI (stands speechless and confused, her eyes bent on the ground; at last she falls at the QUEEN's feet).

Gracious queen!

Have pity on me! Let me--let me not,-- For heaven's sake, let me not be sacrificed.

QUEEN.

Be sacrificed! I need no more. Arise! 'Tis a hard fortune to be sacrificed.

I do believe you. Rise. And is it long Since you rejected Gomez' suit?

EBOLI.

Some months-- Before Prince Carlos came from Alcala.

QUEEN (starts and looks at her with an inquisitive glance). Have you tried well the grounds of your refusal?

EBOLI (with energy).

It cannot be, my queen, no, never, never,-- For a thousand reasons, never!

QUEEN.

One's enough, You do not love him. That suffices me. Now let it pass.

[To her other ladies.

I have not seen the Infanta Yet this morning. Pray bring her, marchioness.

OLIVAREZ (looking at the clock). It is not yet the hour, your majesty.

QUEEN.

Not yet the hour for me to be a mother!

That's somewhat hard. Forget not, then, to tell me When the right hour does come.

[A page enters and whispers to the first lady, who thereupon turns to the QUEEN.

OLIVAREZ.

The Marquis Posa!

May it please your majesty.

QUEEN.

The Marquis Posa!

OLIVAREZ.

He comes from France, and from the Netherlands, And craves the honor to present some letters Intrusted to him by your royal mother.

QUEEN.

Is this allowed? OLIVAREZ (hesitating).

A case so unforeseen Is not provided for in my instructions. When a Castilian grandee, with despatches From foreign courts, shall in her garden find The Queen of Spain, and tender them----

QUEEN.

Enough! I'll venture, then, on mine own proper peril.

OLIVAREZ.

May I, your majesty, withdraw the while?

QUEEN.

E'en as you please, good duchess!

[Exit the DUCHESS, the QUEEN gives the PAGE a sign, who thereupon retires.

SCENE IV.

The QUEEN, PRINCESS EBOLI, MARCHIONESS OF MONDECAR,n and

MARQUIS OF POSA.

QUEEN.

I bid you welcome, sir, to Spanish ground!

MARQUIS.

Ground which I never with so just a pride Hailed for the country of my sires as now.

QUEEN (to the two ladies).

The Marquis Posa, ladies, who at Rheims Coped with my father in the lists, and made My colors thrice victorious; the first

That made me feel how proud a thing it was To be the Queen of Spain and Spanish men.

[Turning to the MARQUIS.

When we last parted in the Louvre, Sir, You scarcely dreamed that I should ever be Your hostess in Castile.

MARQUIS.

Most true, my liege!

For at that time I never could have dreamed That France should lose to us the only thing We envied her possessing.

QUEEN.

How, proud Spaniard!

The only thing! And you can venture this-- This to a daughter of the house of Valois!

MARQUIS.

I venture now to say it, gracious queen,

Since now you are our own.

QUEEN.

Your journey hither Has led you, as I hear, through France. What news Have you brought with you from my honored mother And from my dearest brothers?

MARQUIS (handing letters).

I left your royal mother sick at heart, Bereft of every joy save only this, To know her daughter happy on the throne Of our imperial Spain.

QUEEN.

Could she be aught But happy in the dear remembrances Of relatives so kind--in the sweet thoughts Of the old time when--Sir, you've visited Full many a court in these your various travels, And seen strange lands and customs manifold; And now, they say, you mean to keep at home A greater prince in your retired domain Than is King Philip on his throne--a freer. You're a philosopher; but much I doubt

If our Madrid will please you. We are so-- So quiet in Madrid.

MARQUIS.

And that is more Than all the rest of Europe has to boast.

I've heard as much. But all this world's concerns Are well-nigh blotted from my memory.

[To PRINCESS EBOLI.

Princess, methinks I see a hyacinth

Yonder in bloom. Wilt bring it to me, sweet?

[The PRINCESS goes towards the palace, the QUEEN softly to the MARQUIS.

I'm much mistaken, sir, or your arrival Has made one heart more happy here at court.

MARQUIS.

I have found a sad one--one that in this world A ray of sunshine----

EBOLI.

As this gentleman Has seen so many countries, he, no doubt, Has much of note to tell us.

MARQUIS.

Doubtless, and To seek adventures is a knight's first duty-- But his most sacred is to shield the fair.

MONDECAR.

From giants! But there are no giants now!

MARQUIS.

Power is a giant ever to the weak. The chevalier says well. There still are giants; But there are knights no more.

MARQUIS.

Not long ago, On my return from Naples, I became The witness of a very touching story, Which ties of friendship almost make my own Were I not fearful its recital might Fatigue your majesty----

QUEEN.

Have I a choice?

The princess is not to be lightly balked. Proceed. I too, sir, love a story dearly.

MARQUIS.

Two noble houses in Mirandola, Weary of jealousies and deadly feuds, Transmitted down from Guelphs and Ghibellines, Through centuries of hate, from sire to son, Resolved to ratify a lasting peace By the sweet ministry of nuptial ties. Fernando, nephew of the great Pietro, And fair Matilda, old Colonna's child, Were chosen to cement this holy bond. Nature had never for each other formed Two fairer hearts. And never had the world Approved a wiser or a happier choice.

Still had the youth adored his lovely bride In the dull limner's portraiture alone.

How thrilled his heart, then, in the hope to find The truth of all that e'en his fondest dreams Had scarcely dared to credit in her picture! In Padua, where his studies held him bound; Fernando panted for the joyful hour, When he might murmur at Matilda's feet The first pure homage of his fervent love.

[The QUEEN grows more attentive; the MARQUIS continues, after a short pause, addressing himself chiefly to PRINCESS EBOLI.

Meanwhile the sudden death of Pietro's wife Had left him free to wed. With the hot glow Of youthful blood the hoary lover drinks The fame that reached him of Matilda's charms. He comes--he sees--he loves! The new desire Stifles the voice of nature in his heart.

The uncle woos his nephew's destined bride, And at the altar consecrates his theft.

QUEEN.

And what did then Fernando?

MARQUIS.

On the wings Of Jove, unconscious of the fearful change, Delirious with the promised joy, he speeds Back to Mirandola. His flying steed

By starlight gains the gate. Tumultuous sounds Of music, dance, and jocund revelry

Ring from the walls of the illumined palace. With faltering steps he mounts the stair; and now Behold him in the crowded nuptial hall, Unrecognized! Amid the reeling guests Pietro sat. An angel at his side-- An angel, whom he knows, and who to him Even in his dreams, seemed ne'er so beautiful.

A single glance revealed what once was his-- Revealed what now was lost to him forever.

EBOLI.

O poor Fernando!

QUEEN.

Surely, sir, your tale Is ended? Nay, it must be.

MARQUIS.

No, not quite.

QUEEN.

Did you not say Fernando was your friend?

MARQUIS.

I have no dearer in the world.

EBOLI.

But pray Proceed, sir, with your story.

MARQUIS.

Nay, the rest Is very sad--and to recall it sets My sorrow fresh abroach. Spare me the sequel. [A general silence.

QUEEN (turning to the PRINCESS EBOLI). Surely the time is come to see my daughter, I prithee, princess, bring her to me now!

[The PRINCESS withdraws. The MARQUIS beckons a Page. The QUEEN opens the letters, and appears surprised. The MARQUIS talks with MARCHIONESS MONDECAR. The QUEEN having read the letters, turns to the MARQUIS with a penetrating look.

QUEEN.

You have not spoken of Matilda! She Haply was ignorant of Fernando's grief?

MARQUIS.

Matilda's heart has no one fathomed yet-- Great souls endure in silence.

QUEEN.

You look around you. Who is it you seek?

MARQUIS.

Just then the thought came over me, how one, Whose name I dare not mention, would rejoice, Stood he where I do now.

QUEEN.

And who's to blame, That he does not?

MARQUIS (interrupting her eagerly). My liege! And dare I venture

To interpret thee, as fain I would? He'd find

Forgiveness, then, if now he should appear.

QUEEN (alarmed).

Now, marquis, now? What do you mean by this?

MARQUIS.

Might he, then, hope?

QUEEN.

You terrify me, marquis. Surely he will not----

MARQUIS.

He is here already.

SCENE V.

The QUEEN, CARLOS, MARQUIS POSA, MARCHIONESS MONDECAR.

The two latter go towards the avenue.

CARLOS (on his knees before the QUEEN). At length 'tis come--the happy moment's come, And Charles may touch this all-beloved hand.

QUEEN.

What headlong folly's this? And dare you break Into my presence thus? Arise, rash man!

We are observed; my suite are close at hand.

CARLOS.

I will not rise. Here will I kneel forever, Here will I lie enchanted at your feet,

And grow to the dear ground you tread on?

QUEEN.

Madman! To what rude boldness my indulgence leads! Know you, it is the queen, your mother, sir, Whom you address in such presumptuous strain?

Know, that myself will to the king report This bold intrusion----

CARLOS.

And that I must die!

Let them come here, and drag me to the scaffold! A moment spent in paradise like this Is not too dearly purchased by a life.

QUEEN.

But then your queen? CARLOS (rising).

O God, I'll go, I'll go!

Can I refuse to bend to that appeal?

I am your very plaything. Mother, mother, A sign, a transient glance, one broken word From those dear lips can bid me live or die.

What would you more? Is there beneath the sun One thing I would not haste to sacrifice

To meet your lightest wish?

QUEEN.

Then fly!

CARLOS.

God!

QUEEN.

With tears I do conjure you, Carlos, fly! I ask no more. O fly! before my court, My guards, detecting us alone together,

Bear the dread tidings to your father's ear.

CARLOS.

I bide my doom, or be it life or death.

Have I staked every hope on this one moment, Which gives thee to me thus at length alone, That idle fears should balk me of my purpose? No, queen! The world may round its axis roll A hundred thousand times, ere chance again Yield to my prayers a moment such as this.

QUEEN.

It never shall to all eternity.

Unhappy man! What would you ask of me?

CARLOS.

Heaven is my witness, queen, how I have struggled, Struggled as mortal never did before,

But all in vain! My manhood fails--I yield.

QUEEN.

No more of this--for my sake--for my peace.

CARLOS.

You were mine own,--in face of all the world,-- Affianced to me by two mighty crowns,

By heaven and nature plighted as my bride, But Philip, cruel Philip, stole you from me!

QUEEN.

He is your father?

CARLOS.

And he is your husband!

QUEEN.

And gives to you for an inheritance, The mightiest monarchy in all the world.

CARLOS.

And you, as mother!

QUEEN.

Mighty heavens! You rave!

CARLOS.

And is he even conscious of his treasure? Hath he a heart to feel and value yours?

I'll not complain--no, no, I will forget, How happy, past all utterance, I might Have been with you,--if he were only so. But he is not--there, there, the anguish lies! He is not, and he never--never can be.

Oh, you have robbed me of my paradise, Only to blast it in King Philip's arms!

QUEEN.

Horrible thought!

CARLOS.

Oh, yes, right well I know Who 'twas that knit this ill-starred marriage up. I know how Philip loves, and how he wooed.

What are you in this kingdom--tell me, what? Regent, belike! Oh, no! If such you were,

How could fell Alvas act their murderous deeds, Or Flanders bleed a martyr for her faith?

Are you even Philip's wife? Impossible,-- Beyond belief. A wife doth still possess

Her husband's heart. To whom doth his belong? If ever, perchance, in some hot feverish mood, He yields to gentler impulse, begs he not Forgiveness of his sceptre and gray hairs?

QUEEN.

Who told you that my lot, at Philip's side Was one for men to pity?

CARLOS.

My own heart!

Which feels, with burning pangs, how at my side It had been to be envied.

24

QUEEN.

Thou vain man!

What if my heart should tell me the reverse? How, sir, if Philip's watchful tenderness, The looks that silently proclaim his love, Touched me more deeply than his haughty son's Presumptuous eloquence? What, if an old man's Matured esteem----

CARLOS.

That makes a difference! Then, Why then, forgiveness!--I'd no thought of this; I had no thought that you could love the king.

QUEEN.

To honor him's my pleasure and my wish.

CARLOS.

Then you have never loved?

QUEEN.

Singular question!

CARLOS.

Then you have never loved?

QUEEN.

I love no longer!

CARLOS.

Because your heart forbids it, or your oath?

QUEEN.

Leave me; nor never touch this theme again.

CARLOS.

Because your oath forbids it, or your heart?

QUEEN.

Because my duty--but, alas, alas! To what avails this scrutiny of fate, Which we must both obey?

CARLOS.

Must--must obey?

QUEEN.

What means this solemn tone?

CARLOS.

Thus much it means That Carlos is not one to yield to must Where he hath power to will! It means, besides, 'That Carlos is not minded to live on, The most unhappy man in all his realm, When it would only cost the overthrow Of Spanish laws to be the happiest.

QUEEN.

Do I interpret rightly? Still you hope? Dare you hope on, when all is lost forever?

CARLOS.

I look on naught as lost--except the dead.

QUEEN.

For me--your mother, do you dare to hope?

[She fixes a penetrating look on him, then continues with dignity and earnestness.

And yet why not? A new elected monarch Can do far more--make bonfires of the laws His father left--o'erthrow his monuments-- Nay, more than this--for what shall hinder him?-- Drag from his tomb, in the Escurial,

The sacred corpse of his departed sire, Make it a public spectacle, and scatter Forth to the winds his desecrated dust. And then, at last, to fill the measure up----

CARLOS.

Merciful heavens, finish not the picture!

QUEEN.

End all by wedding with his mother.

CARLOS.

Oh!

Accursed son!

[He remains for some time paralyzed and speechless. Yes, now 'tis out, 'tis out!

I see it clear as day. Oh, would it had Been veiled from me in everlasting darkness! Yes, thou art gone from me--gone--gone forever. The die is cast; and thou art lost to me.

Oh, in that thought lies hell; and a hell, too, Lies in the other thought, to call thee mine. Oh, misery! I can bear my fate no longer,

My very heart-strings strain as they would burst.

QUEEN.

Alas, alas! dear Charles, I feel it all, The nameless pang that rages in your breast; Your pangs are infinite, as is your love, And infinite as both will be the glory Of overmastering both. Up, be a man, Wrestle with them boldly. The prize is worthy Of a young warrior's high, heroic heart; Worthy of him in whom the virtues flow Of a long ancestry of mighty kings.

Courage! my noble prince! Great Charles's grandson Begins the contest with undaunted heart, Where sons of meaner men would yield at once.

CARLOS.

Too late, too late! O God, it is too late!

QUEEN.

Too late to be a man! O Carlos, Carlos! How nobly shows our virtue when the heart Breaks in its exercise! The hand of Heaven Has set you up on high,--far higher, prince, Than millions of your brethren. All she took From others she bestowed with partial hand On thee, her favorite; and millions ask, What was your merit, thus before your birth To be endowed so far above mankind?

Up, then, and justify the ways of Heaven; Deserve to take the lead of all the world, And make a sacrifice ne'er made before.

CARLOS.

I will, I will; I have a giant's strength

To win your favor; but to lose you, none.

QUEEN.

Confess, my Carlos, I have harshly read thee; It is but spoken, and waywardness, and pride, Attract you thus so madly to your mother!

The heart you lavish on myself belongs To the great empire you one day shall rule. Look that you sport not with your sacred trust! Love is your high vocation; until now It hath been wrongly bent upon your mother: Oh, lead it back upon your future realms, And so, instead of the fell stings of conscience, Enjoy the bliss of being more than man. Elizabeth has been your earliest love, Your second must be Spain. How gladly, Carlos, Will I give place to this more worthy choice!

CARLOS (overpowered by emotion, throws himself at her feet). How great thou art, my angel! Yes, I'll do All, all thou canst desire. So let it be. [He rises.

Here in the sight of heaven I stand and swear-- I swear to thee, eternal--no, great Heaven!-- Eternal silence only,--not oblivion!

QUEEN.

How can I ask from you what I myself Am not disposed to grant?

MARQUIS (hastening from the alley). The king!

QUEEN.

Oh God!

MARQUIS.

Away, away! fly from these precincts, prince!

QUEEN.

His jealousy is dreadful--should he see you----

CARLOS.

I'll stay.

QUEEN.

And who will be the victim then?

CARLOS (seizing the MARQUIS by the arm). Away, away! Come, Roderigo, come!

[Goes and returns. What may I hope to carry hence with me?

QUEEN.

Your mother's friendship.

CARLOS.

Friendship! Mother!

QUEEN.

And

These tears with it--they're from the Netherlands.

[She gives him some letters. Exit CARLOS with the MARQUIS. The QUEEN looks restlessly round in search of her ladies, who are nowhere to be seen. As she is about to retire up, the KING enters.

SCENE VI.

The KING, the QUEEN, DUKE ALVA, COUNT LERMA, DOMINGO,

LADIES, GRANDEES, who remain at a little distance.

KING.

How, madam, alone; not even one of all

Your ladies in attendance? Strange! Where are they?

QUEEN.

My gracious lord!

KING.

Why thus alone, I say? [To his attendants.

I'll take a strict account of this neglect.

'Tis not to be forgiven. Who has the charge Of waiting on your majesty to-day?

QUEEN.

Oh, be not angry! Good, my lord, 'tis I Myself that am to blame--at my request

The Princess Eboli went hence but now.

KING.

At your request!

QUEEN.

To call the nurse to me, With the Infanta, whom I longed to see.

KING.

And was your retinue dismissed for that? This only clears the lady first in waiting. Where was the second?

MONDECAR (who has returned and mixed with the other ladies, steps forward).

Your majesty, I feel I am to blame for this.

KING.

You are, and so I give you ten years to reflect upon it, At a most tranquil distance from Madrid.

[The MARCHIONESS steps back weeping. General silence. The bystanders all look in confusion towards the QUEEN.

QUEEN.

What weep you for, dear marchioness?

[To the KING. If I

Have erred, my gracious liege, the crown I wear, And which I never sought, should save my blushes Is there a law in this your kingdom, sire, To summon monarch's daughters to the bar? Does force alone restrain your Spanish ladies? Or need they stronger safeguard than their virtue? Now pardon me, my liege; 'tis not my wont To send my ladies, who have served me still With smiling cheerfulness, away in tears. Here, Mondecar.

[She takes off her girdle and presents it to the MARCHIONESS. You have displeased the king, Not me. Take this remembrance of my favor, And of this hour. I'd have you quit the kingdom. You have only erred in Spain. In my dear France, All men are glad to wipe such tears away. And must I ever be reminded thus? In my dear France it had been otherwise.

[Leaning on the MARCHIONESS and covering her face.

KING.

Can a reproach, that in my love had birth, Afflict you so? A word so trouble you, Which the most anxious tenderness did prompt?

[He turns towards the GEANDEES.

Here stand the assembled vassals of my throne. Did ever sleep descend upon these eyes, Till at the close of the returning day

I've pondered, how the hearts of all my subjects Were beating 'neath the furthest cope of heaven? And should I feel more anxious for my throne Than for the partner of my bosom? No!

My sword and Alva can protect my people, My eye alone assures thy love.

QUEEN.

My liege,

If that I have offended----

KING.

I am called The richest monarch in the Christian world; The sun in my dominions never sets.

All this another hath possessed before, And many another will possess hereafter.

That is mine own. All that the monarch hath Belongs to chance--Elizabeth to Philip.

This is the point in which I feel I'm mortal.

QUEEN.

What fear you, sire?

KING.

Should these gray hairs not fear?

But the same instant that my fear begins It dies away forever.

[To the grandees. I run over The nobles of my court and miss the foremost. Where is my son, Don Carlos? [No one answers.

He begins To give me cause of fear. He shuns my presence Since he came back from school at Alcala.

His blood is hot. Why is his look so cold? His bearing all so stately and reserved? Be watchful, duke, I charge you.

ALVA.

So I am: Long as a heart against this corslet beats, So long may Philip slumber undisturbed; And as God's cherub guards the gates of heaven So doth Duke Alva guard your royal throne.

LERMA.

Dare I, in all humility, presume To oppose the judgment of earth's wisest king? Too deeply I revere his gracious sire To judge the son so harshly. I fear much From his hot blood, but nothing from his heart.

KING.

Lerma, your speech is fair to soothe the father, But Alva here will be the monarch's shield-- No more of this.

[Turning to his suite. Now speed we to Madrid, Our royal duties summon us. The plague Of heresy is rife among my people; Rebellion stalks within my Netherlands-- The times are imminent. We must arrest These erring spirits by some dread example. The solemn oath which every Christian king Hath sworn to keep I will redeem to-morrow. 'Twill be a day of doom unparalleled.

Our court is bidden to the festival.

[He leads off the QUEEN, the rest follow.

SCENE VII.

DON CARLOS (with letters in his hand), and MARQUIS POSA enter from opposite sides.

CARLOS.

I am resolved--Flanders shall yet be saved: So runs her suit, and that's enough for me!

MARQUIS.

There's not another moment to be lost: 'Tis said Duke Alva in the cabinet Is named already as the governor.

CARLOS.

Betimes to-morrow will I see the king And ask this office for myself. It is The first request I ever made to him, And he can scarce refuse. My presence here Has long been irksome to him. He will grasp This fair pretence my absence to secure.

And shall I confess to thee, Roderigo?

My hopes go further. Face to face with him, 'Tis possible the pleading of a son

May reinstate him in his father's favor.

He ne'er hath heard the voice of nature speak; Then let me try for once, my Roderigo,

What power she hath when breathing from my lips.

MARQUIS.

Now do I hear my Carlos' voice once more; Now are you all yourself again!

SCENE VIII.

The preceding. COUNT LERMA.

COUNT.

Your grace, His majesty has left Aranjuez; And I am bidden----

CARLOS.

Very well, my lord-- I shall overtake the king----

MARQUIS (affecting to take leave with ceremony). Your highness, then, Has nothing further to intrust to me?

CARLOS.

Nothing. A pleasant journey to Madrid!

You may, hereafter, tell me more of Flanders. [To LERMA, who is waiting for him.

Proceed, my lord! I'll follow thee anon.

SCENE IX.

DON CARLOS, MARQUIS POSA. CARLOS.

I understood thy hint, and thank thee for it. A stranger's presence can alone excuse

This forced and measured tone. Are we not brothers?

In future, let this puppet-play of rank

Be banished from our friendship. Think that we Had met at some gay masking festival,

Thou in the habit of a slave, and I Robed, for a jest, in the imperial purple.

Throughout the revel we respect the cheat, And play our parts with sportive earnestness, Tripping it gayly with the merry throng;

But should thy Carlos beckon through his mask, Thou'dst press his hand in silence as he passed, And we should be as one.

MARQUIS.

The dream's divine!

But are you sure that it will last forever? Is Carlos, then, so certain of himself

As to despise the charms of boundless sway? A day will come--an all-important day-- When this heroic mind--I warn you now-- Will sink o'erwhelmed by too severe a test.

Don Philip dies; and Carlos mounts the throne, The mightiest throne in Christendom. How vast The gulf that yawns betwixt mankind and him-- A god to-day, who yesterday was man!

Steeled to all human weakness--to the voice Of heavenly duty deaf. Humanity-- To-day a word of import in his ear-- Barters itself, and grovels 'mid the throng Of gaping parasites; his sympathy For human woe is turned to cold neglect, His virtue sunk in loose voluptuous joys. Peru supplies him riches for his folly, His court engenders devils for his vices.

Lulled in this heaven the work of crafty slaves, He sleeps a charmed sleep; and while his dream Endures his godhead lasts. And woe to him Who'd break in pity this lethargic trance!

What could Roderigo do? Friendship is true, And bold as true. But her bright flashing beams Were much too fierce for sickly majesty:

You would not brook a subject's stern appeal, Nor I a monarch's pride!

CARLOS.

Tearful and true, Thy portraiture of monarchs. Yes--thou'rt right, But 'tis their lusts that thus corrupt their hearts, And hurry them to vice. I still am pure.

A youth scarce numbering three-and-twenty years. What thousands waste in riotous delights, Without remorse--the mind's more precious part-- The bloom and strength of manhood--I have kept, Hoarding their treasures for the future king.

What could unseat my Posa from my heart, If woman fail to do it?

MARQUIS.

I, myself!

Say, could I love you, Carlos, warm as now, If I must fear you?

CARLOS.

That will never be.

What need hast thou of me? What cause hast thou To stoop thy knee, a suppliant at the throne?

Does gold allure thee? Thou'rt a richer subject Than I shall be a king! Dost covet honors?

E'en in thy youth, fame's brimming chalice stood Full in thy grasp--thou flung'st the toy away. Which of us, then, must be the other's debtor, And which the creditor? Thou standest mute. Dost tremble for the trial? Art thou, then, Uncertain of thyself?

MARQUIS.

Carlos, I yield! Here is my band.

CARLOS.

Is it mine own?

MARQUIS.

Forever-- In the most pregnant meaning of the word!

CARLOS.

And wilt thou prove hereafter to the king As true and warm as to the prince to-day?

MARQUIS.

I swear!

CARLOS.

And when round my unguarded heart The serpent flattery winds its subtle coil, Should e'er these eyes of mine forget the tears They once were wont to shed; or should these ears Be closed to mercy's plea,--say, wilt thou, then, The fearless guardian of my virtue, throw Thine iron grasp upon me, and call up My genius by its mighty name?

MARQUIS.

I will.

CARLOS.

And now one other favor let me beg.

Do call me thou! Long have I envied this Dear privilege of friendship to thine equals. The brother's thou beguiles my ear, my heart, With sweet suggestions of equality.

Nay, no reply:--I guess what thou wouldst say-- To thee this seems a trifle--but to me, A monarch's son, 'tis much. Say, wilt thou be A brother to me?

MARQUIS.

Yes; thy brother, yes!

CARLOS.

Now to the king--my fears are at an end. Thus, arm-in-arm with thee, I dare defy The universal world into the lists.

[Exeunt.

ACT II.

SCENE I.

The royal palace at Madrid.

KING PHILIP under a canopy; DUKE ALVA at some distance, with his head covered; CARLOS.

CARLOS.

The kingdom takes precedence--willingly Doth Carlos to the minister give place--

He speaks for Spain; I am but of the household. [Bows and steps backward.

KING.

The duke remains--the Infanta may proceed.

CARLOS (turning to ALVA).

Then must I put it to your honor, sir, To yield my father for a while to me. A son, you know, may to a father's ear Unbosom much, in fulness of his heart, That not befits a stranger's ear. The king Shall not be taken from you, sir--I seek The father only for one little hour.

KING.

Here stands his friend.

CARLOS.

And have I e'er deserved

To think the duke should be a friend of mine?

KING.

Or tried to make him one? I scarce can love Those sons who choose more wisely than their fathers.

CARLOS.

And can Duke Alva's knightly spirit brook To look on such a scene? Now, as I live, I would not play the busy meddler's part, Who thrusts himself, unasked, 'twixt sire and son, And there intrudes without a blush, condemned By his own conscious insignificance,

No, not, by heaven, to win a diadem!

KING (rising, with an angry look at the Prince). Retire, my lord!

[ALVA goes to the principal door, through which CARLOS had entered, the KING points to the other.

No, to the cabinet, Until I call you.

SCENE II.

KING PHILIP. DON CARLOS.

CARLOS (as soon as the DUKE has left the apartment, advances to the KING, throws himself at his feet, and then, with great emotion). My father once again!

Thanks, endless thanks, for this unwonted favor!

Your hand, my father! O delightful day!

The rapture of this kiss has long been strange To your poor Carlos. Wherefore have I been Shut from my father's heart? What have I done?

KING.

Carlos, thou art a novice in these arts-- Forbear, I like them not----

CARLOS (rising).

And is it so?

I hear your courtiers in those words, my father! All is not well, by heaven, all is not true, That a priest says, and a priest's creatures plot. I am not wicked, father; ardent blood Is all my failing;--all my crime is youth;-- Wicked I am not--no, in truth, not wicked;-- Though many an impulse wild assails my heart, Yet is it still untainted.

KING.

Ay, 'tis pure-- I know it--like thy prayers----

CARLOS.

Now, then, or never!

We are, for once, alone--the barrier Of courtly form, that severed sire and son Has fallen! Now a golden ray of hope Illumes my soul--a sweet presentment Pervades my heart--and heaven itself inclines, With choirs of joyous angels, to the earth, And full of soft emotion, the thrice blest Looks down upon this great, this glorious scene! Pardon, my father!

[He falls on his knees before him.

KING.

Rise, and leave me.

CARLOS.

Father!

KING (tearing himself from him). This trifling grows too bold.

CARLOS.

A son's devotion Too bold! Alas!

KING.

And, to crown all, in tears!

Degraded boy! Away, and quit my sight!

CARLOS.

Now, then, or never!--pardon, O my father!

KING.

Away, and leave my sight! Return to me Disgraced, defeated, from the battle-field, Thy sire shall meet thee with extended arms: But thus in tears, I spurn thee from my feet. A coward's guilt alone should wash its stains In such ignoble streams. The man who weeps Without a blush will ne'er want cause for tears!

CARLOS.

Who is this man? By what mistake of nature Has he thus strayed amongst mankind? A tear Is man's unerring, lasting attribute.

Whose eye is dry was ne'er of woman born! Oh, teach the eye that ne'er hath overflowed, The timely science of a tear--thou'lt need The moist relief in some dark hour of woo.

KING.

Think'st thou to shake thy father's strong mistrust With specious words?

CARLOS.

Mistrust! Then I'll remove it.

Here will I hang upon my father's breast, Strain at his heart with vigor, till each shred

Of that mistrust, which, with a rock's endurance, Clings firmly round it, piecemeal fall away.

And who are they who drive me from the king-- My father's favor? What requital hath

A monk to give a father for a son?

What compensation can the duke supply For a deserted and a childless age?

Would'st thou be loved? Here in this bosom springs A fresher, purer fountain, than e'er flowed From those dark, stagnant, muddy reservoirs, Which Philip's gold must first unlock.

KING.

No more, Presuming boy! For know the hearts thou slanderest Are the approved, true servants of my choice.

'Tis meet that thou do honor to them.

CARLOS.

Never!

I know my worth--all that your Alva dares-- That, and much more, can Carlos. What cares he, A hireling! for the welfare of the realm That never can be his? What careth he If Philip's hair grow gray with hoary age?

Your Carlos would have loved you:--Oh, I dread To think that you the royal throne must fill Deserted and alone.

KING (seemingly struck by this idea, stands in deep thought; after a pause).

I am alone!

CARLOS (approaching him with eagerness). You have been so till now. Hate me no more, And I will love you dearly as a son:

But hate me now no longer! Oh, how sweet, Divinely sweet it is to feel our being Reflected in another's beauteous soul; To see our joys gladden another's cheek, Our pains bring anguish to another's bosom, Our sorrows fill another's eye with tears!

How sweet, how glorious is it, hand in hand, With a dear child, in inmost soul beloved, To tread once more the rosy paths of youth, And dream life's fond illusions o'er again!

How proud to live through endless centuries Immortal in the virtues of a son; How sweet to plant what his dear hand shall reap; To gather what will yield him rich return, And guess how high his thanks will one day rise! My father of this early paradise

Your monks most wisely speak not. KING (not without emotion).

Oh, my son, Thou hast condemned thyself in painting thus A bliss this heart hath ne'er enjoyed from thee.

CARLOS.

The Omniscient be my judge! You till this hour Have still debarred me from your heart, and all Participation in your royal cares.

The heir of Spain has been a very stranger In Spanish land--a prisoner in the realm Where he must one day rule. Say, was this just, Or kind? And often have I blushed for shame,

And stood with eyes abashed, to learn perchance From foreign envoys, or the general rumor, Thy courtly doings at Aranjuez.

KING.

Thy blood flows far too hotly in thy veins. Thou would'st but ruin all.

CARLOS.

But try me, father.

'Tis true my blood flows hotly in my veins. Full three-and-twenty years I now have lived, And naught achieved for immortality.

I am aroused--I feel my inward powers-- My title to the throne arouses me From slumber, like an angry creditor; And all the misspent hours of early youth, Like debts of honor, clamor in mine ears.

It comes at length, the glorious moment comes That claims full interest on the intrusted talent. The annals of the world, ancestral fame, And glory's echoing trumpet urge me on. Now is the blessed hour at length arrived That opens wide to me the list of honor. My king, my father! dare I utter now The suit which led me hither?

KING.

Still a suit? Unfold it.

CARLOS.

The rebellion in Brabant Increases to a height--the traitor's madness By stern, but prudent, vigor must be met. The duke, to quell the wild enthusiasm, Invested with the sovereign's power, will lead An army into Flanders. Oh, how full Of glory is such office! and how suited To open wide the temple of renown To me, your son! To my hand, then, O king, Intrust the army; in thy Flemish lands I am well loved, and I will freely gage My life for their fidelity and truth.

KING.

Thou speakest like a dreamer. This high office Demands a man--and not a stripling's arm.

CARLOS.

It but demands a human being, father:

And that is what Duke Alva ne'er hath been.

KING.

Terror alone can tie rebellion's hands: Humanity were madness. Thy soft soul Is tender, son: they'll tremble at the duke. Desist from thy request.

CARLOS.

Despatch me, sire, To Flanders with the army--dare rely E'en on my tender soul. The name of prince, The royal name emblazoned on my standard, Conquers where Alva's butchers but dismay. Here on my knees I crave it--this the first Petition of my life. Trust Flanders to me.

KING (contemplating CARLOS with a piercing look). Trust my best army to thy thirst for rule, And put a dagger in my murderer's hand!

CARLOS.

Great God! and is this all--is this the fruit Of a momentous hour so long desired!

[After some thought, in a milder tone.

Oh, speak to me more kindly--send me not Thus comfortless away--dismiss me not With this afflicting answer, oh, my father! Use me more tenderly, indeed, I need it.

This is the last resource of wild despair-- It conquers every power of firm resolve To beat it as a man--this deep contempt-- My every suit denied: Let me away-- Unheard and foiled in all my fondest hopes, I take my leave. Now Alva and Domingo May proudly sit in triumph where your son Lies weeping in the dust. Your crowd of courtiers, And your long train of cringing, trembling nobles, Your tribe of sallow monks, so deadly pale, All witnessed how you granted me this audience. Let me not be disgraced. Oh, strike me not With this most deadly wound--nor lay me bare To sneering insolence of menial taunts! "That strangers riot on your bounty, whilst Carlos, your son, may supplicate in vain." And as a pledge that you would have me honored, Despatch me straight to Flanders with the army.

KING.

Urge thy request no farther--as thou wouldst Avoid the king's displeasure.

CARLOS.

I must brave My king's displeasure, and prefer my suit Once more, it is the last. Trust Flanders to me! I must away from Spain. To linger here Is to draw breath beneath the headsman's axe: The air lies heavy on me in Madrid Like murder on a guilty soul--a change, An instant change of clime alone can cure me. If you would save my life, despatch me straight Without delay to Flanders.

KING (with affected coldness). Invalids, Like thee, my son--need not be tended close, And ever watched by the physician's eye-- Thou stayest in Spain--the duke will go to Flanders.

CARLOS (wildly).

Assist me, ye good angels! KING (starting).

Hold, what mean Those looks so wild?

CARLOS.

Father, do you abide Immovably by this determination?

KING.

It was the king's.

CARLOS.

Then my commission's done. [Exit in violent emotion.

SCENE III.

King, sunk in gloomy contemplation, walks a few steps up and down; Alva approaches with embarrassment.

KING.

Hold yourself ready to depart for Brussels Upon a moment's notice.

ALVA.

All is prepared, my liege.

KING.

And your credentials

Lie ready sealed within my cabinet,-- Meanwhile obtain an audience of the queen, And bid the prince farewell.

ALVA.

As I came in

I met him with a look of frenzy wild Quitting the chamber; and your majesty

Is strangely moved, methinks, and bears the marks Of deep excitement--can it be the theme Of your discourse----

KING.

Concerned the Duke of Alva.

[The KING keeps his eye steadfastly fixed on him. I'm pleased that Carlos hates my councillors, But I'm disturbed that he despises them.

[ALVA, coloring deeply, is about to speak. No answer now: propitiate the prince.

ALVA.

Sire!

KING.

Tell me who it was that warned me first Of my son's dark designs? I listened then To you, and not to him. I will have proof. And for the future, mark me, Carlos stands Nearer the throne--now duke--you may retire.

[*The* KING *retires into his cabinet. Exit* DUKE *by another door.*

SCENE IV.

The antechamber to the QUEEN'S apartments. DON CARLOS enters in conversation with a PAGE. The attendants retire at his approach.

CARLOS.

For me this letter? And a key! How's this? And both delivered with such mystery!

Come nearer, boy:--from whom didst thou receive them?

PAGE (mysteriously).

It seemed to me the lady would be guessed Rather than be described.

CARLOS (starting). The lady, what!

Who art thou, boy?

[Looking earnestly at the PAGE.

PAGE.

A page that serves the queen.

CARLOS (affrighted, putting his hand to the PAGE's mouth). Hold, on your life! I know enough: no more.

[He tears open the letter hastily, and retires to read it; meanwhile DUKE ALVA comes, and passing the Prince, goes unperceived by him into the QUEEN'S apartment, CARLOS trembles violently and changes color; when he has read the letter he remains a long time speechless, his eyes steadfastly fixed on it; at last he turns to the PAGE.

She gave you this herself?

PAGE.

With her own hands.

CARLOS.

She gave this letter to you then herself?

Deceive me not: I ne'er have seen her writing, And I must credit thee, if thou canst swear it; But if thy tale be false, confess it straight, Nor put this fraud on me.

PAGE.

This fraud, on whom?

CARLOS (looking once more at the letter, then at the PAGE with doubt and earnestness).

Your parents--are they living? and your father-- Serves he the king? Is he a Spaniard born?

PAGE.

He fell a colonel on St. Quentin's field, Served in the cavalry of Savoy's duke-- His name Alonzo, Count of Henarez.

CARLOS (taking his hand, and looking fixedly in his eyes). The king gave you this letter?

PAGE (with emotion). Gracious prince, Have I deserved these doubts?

CARLOS (reading the letter). "This key unlocks The back apartments in the queen's pavilion, The furthest room lies next a cabinet Wherein no listener's foot dare penetrate; Here may the voice of love without restraint Confess those tender feelings, which till now

The heart with silent looks alone hath spoken. The timid lover gains an audience here, And sweet reward repays his secret sorrow." [As if awakening from a reverie.

I am not in a dream, do not rave, This is my right hand, this my sword--and these Are written words. 'Tis true--it is no dream.

I am beloved, I feel I am beloved.

[Unable to contain himself, he rushes hastily through the room, and raises his arms to heaven.

PAGE.

Follow me, prince, and I will lead the way.

CARLOS.

Then let me first collect my scattered thoughts. The alarm of joy still trembles in my bosom.

Did I e'er lift my fondest hopes so high, Or trust my fancy to so bold a flight?

Show me the man can learn thus suddenly To be a god. I am not what I was.

I feel another heaven--another sun

That was not here before. She loves--she loves me!

PAGE (leading him forward).

But this is not the place: prince! you forget.

CARLOS.

The king! My father!

[His arms sink, he casts a timid look around, then collecting himself.

This is dreadful! Yes, You're right, my friend. I thank you: I was not Just then myself. To be compelled to silence, And bury in my heart this mighty bliss, Is terrible!

[Taking the PAGE by the hand, and leading him aside. Now here! What thou hast seen, And what not seen, must be within thy breast Entombed as in the grave. So now depart; I shall not need thy guidance; they must not Surprise us here! Now go. [The PAGE is about to depart. Yet hold, a word!

[The PAGE returns. CARLOS lays his hand on his shoulder, and looks him steadily in the face.

A direful secret hast thou in thy keeping, Which, like a poison of terrific power, Shivers the cup that holds it into atoms. Guard every look of thine, nor let thy head Guess at thy bosom's secret. Be thou like The senseless speaking-trumpet that receives And echoes back the voice, but hears it not. Thou art a boy! Be ever so; continue The pranks of youth. My correspondent chose Her messenger of love with prudent skill! The king will ne'er suspect a serpent here.

PAGE.

And I, my prince, shall feel right proud to know I am one secret richer than the king.

CARLOS.

Vain, foolish boy! 'tis this should make thee tremble. Approach me ever with a cold respect:

Ne'er be induced by idle pride to boast How gracious is the prince! No deadlier sin Canst thou commit, my son, than pleasing me. Whate'er thou hast in future for my ear, Give not to words; intrust not to thy lips, Ne'er on that common high road of the thoughts Permit thy news to travel. Speak with an eye, A finger; I will answer with a look.

The very air, the light, are Philip's creatures, And the deaf walls around are in his pay.

Some one approaches; fly, we'll meet again.

[The QUEEN'S chamber opens, and DUKE ALVA comes out.

PAGE.

Be careful, prince, to find the right apartment. [Exit.

CARLOS.

It is the duke! Fear not, I'll find the way.

SCENE V.

DON CARLOS. DUDE OF ALVA.

ALVA (meeting him).

Two words, most gracious prince.

CARLOS.

Some other time.

[Going.

ALVA.

The place is not the fittest, I confess; Perhaps your royal highness may be pleased To grant me audience in your private chamber.

CARLOS.

For what? And why not here? Only be brief.

ALVA.

The special object which has brought me hither, Is to return your highness lowly thanks

For your good services.

CARLOS.

Thanks to me-- For what? Duke Alva's thanks!

ALVA.

You scarce had left

His majesty, ere I received in form Instructions to depart for Brussels.

CARLOS.

What!

For Brussels!

ALVA.

And to what, most gracious prince, Must I ascribe this favor, but to you-- Your intercession with the king?

Oh, no!

Not in the least to me; but, duke, you travel, So Heaven be with your grace!

ALVA.

And is this all?

It seems, indeed, most strange! And has your highness No further orders, then, to send to Flanders?

CARLOS.

What should I have?

ALVA.

Not long ago, it seemed, The country's fate required your presence.

CARLOS.

How?

But yes, you're right,--it was so formerly; But now this change is better as it is.

ALVA.

I am amazed----

CARLOS.

You are an able general, No one doubts that--envy herself must own it. For me, I'm but a youth--so thought the king.

The king was right, quite right. I see it now Myself, and am content--and so no more.

God speed your journey, as you see, just now My hands are full, and weighty business presses. The rest to-morrow, or whene'er you will, Or when you come from Brussels.

ALVA.

What is this?

CARLOS.

The season favors, and your route will lie Through Milan, Lorraine, Burgundy, and on To Germany! What, Germany? Ay, true, In Germany it was--they know you there. 'Tis April now, May, June,--in July, then, Just so! or, at the latest, soon in August,-- You will arrive in Brussels, and no doubt We soon shall hear of your victorious deeds. You know the way to win our high esteem, And earn the crown of fame.

ALVA

(significantly). Indeed! Condemned By my own conscious insignificance!

CARLOS.

You're sensitive, my lord, and with some cause, I own it was not fair to use a weapon

Against your grace you were unskilled to wield.

ALVA.

Unskilled!

'Tis pity I've no leisure now

To fight this worthy battle fairly out But at some other time, we----

ALVA.

Prince, we both Miscalculate--but still in opposite ways. You, for example, overrate your age By twenty years, whilst on the other band, I, by as many, underrate it----

CARLOS.

Well

ALVA.

And this suggests the thought, how many nights Beside this lovely Lusitanian bride-- Your mother--would the king right gladly give To buy an arm like this, to aid his crown. Full well he knows, far easier is the task To make a monarch than a monarchy; Far easier too, to stock the world with kings Than frame an empire for a king to rule.

CARLOS.

Most true, Duke Alva, yet----

ALVA.

And how much blood, Your subjects' dearest blood, must flow in streams Before two drops could make a king of you.

Most true, by heaven! and in two words comprised, All that the pride of merit has to urge Against the pride of fortune. But the moral-- Now, Duke Alva!

ALVA.

Woe to the nursling babe Of royalty that mocks the careful hand Which fosters it! How calmly it may sleep On the soft cushion of our victories!

The monarch's crown is bright with sparkling gems, But no eye sees the wounds that purchased them.

52

This sword has given our laws to distant realms, Has blazed before the banner of the cross, And in these quarters of the globe has traced Ensanguined furrows for the seed of faith. God was the judge in heaven, and I on earth.

CARLOS.

God, or the devil--it little matters which; Yours was his chosen arm--that stands confessed. And now no more of this. Some thoughts there are Whereof the memory pains me. I respect My father's choice,--my father needs an Alva! But that he needs him is not just the point I envy in him: a great man you are, This may be true, and I well nigh believe it, Only I fear your mission is begun Some thousand years too soon. Alva, methinks, Were just the man to suit the end of time.

Then when the giant insolence of vice Shall have exhausted Heaven's enduring patience, And the rich waving harvest of misdeeds Stand in full ear, and asks a matchless reaper, Then should you fill the post. O God! my paradise! My Flanders! But of this I must not think.

'Tis said you carry with you a full store Of sentences of death already signed.

This shows a prudent foresight! No more need To fear your foes' designs, or secret plots:

Oh, father! ill indeed I've understood thee. Calling thee harsh, to save me from a post, Where Alva's self alone can fitly shine! 'Twas an unerring token of your love.

ALVA.

These words deserve----

CARLOS.

What!

ALVA.

But your birth protects you. CARLOS (seizing his sword).

That calls for blood! Duke, draw your sword! ALVA (slightingly).

On whom?

CARLOS. (pressing upon him). Draw, or I run you through.

ALVA.

Then be it so.

[They fight.

SCENE VI.

The QUEEN, DON CARLOS, DUKE ALVA.

QUEEN (coming from her room alarmed). How! naked swords?

[To the PRINCE in an indignant and commanding tone. Prince Carlos!

CARLOS (agitated at the QUEEN's look, drops his arm, stands motionless, then rushes to the DUKE, and embraces him).

Pardon, duke!

Your pardon, sir! Forget, forgive it all!

[Throws himself in silence at the QUEEN'S feet, then rising suddenly, departs in confusion.

ALVA.

By heaven, 'tis strange!

QUEEN (remains a few moments as if in doubt, then retiring to her apartment).

A word with you, Duke ALVA. [Exit, followed by the DUKE. SCENE VII.

The PRINCESS EBOLI's apartment.

The PRINCESS in a simple, but elegant dress, playing on the lute. The QUEEN's PAGE enters.

PRINCESS (starting up suddenly) He comes!

PAGE (abruptly).

Are you alone? I wonder much

He is not here already; but he must Be here upon the instant.

PRINCESS.

Do you say must!

Then he will come, this much is certain then.

PAGE.

He's close upon my steps. You are beloved, Adored, and with more passionate regard Than mortal ever was, or can be loved.

Oh! what a scene I witnessed!

PRINCESS

(impatiently draws him to her). Quick, you spoke With him! What said he? Tell me straight-- How did he look? what were his words? And say-- Did he appear embarrassed or confused And did he guess who sent the key to him? Be quick! or did he not? He did not guess At all, perhaps! or guessed amiss! Come, speak, How! not a word to answer me? Oh, fie! You never were so dull--so slow before, 'Tis past all patience.

PAGE.

Dearest lady, hear me!

Both key and note I placed within his hands, In the queen's antechamber, and he started And gazed with wonder when I told him that A lady sent me!

PRINCESS.

Did he start? go on!

That's excellent. Proceed, what next ensued?

PAGE.

I would have told him more, but he grew pale, And snatched the letter from my hand, and said With look of deadly menace, he knew all.

He read the letter with confusion through, And straight began to tremble.

PRINCESS.

He knew all! He knew it all? Were those his very words?

PAGE.

He asked me, and again he asked, if you With your own hands had given me the letter?

PRINCESS.

If I? Then did he mention me by name?

PAGE.

By name! no name he mentioned: there might be Listeners, he said, about the palace, who Might to the king disclose it.

PRINCESS

(surprised). Said he that?

PAGE.

He further said, it much concerned the king; Deeply concerned--to know of that same letter.

PRINCESS.

The king! Nay, are you sure you heard him right? The king! Was that the very word he used?

PAGE.

It was. He called it a most perilous secret, And warned me to be strictly on my guard, Never with word or look to give the king Occasion for suspicion.

PRINCESS (after a pause, with astonishment). All agrees!

It can be nothing else--he must have heard The tale--'tis very strange! Who could have told him, I wonder who? The eagle eye of love

Alone could pierce so far. But tell me further-- He read the letter.

PAGE.

Which, he said, conveyed Such bliss as made him tremble, and till then He had not dared to dream of. As he spoke The duke, by evil chance, approached the room, And this compelled us----

PRINCESS (angrily).

What in all the world Could bring the duke to him at such a time? What can detain him? Why appears he not? See how you've been deceived; how truly blest Might he have been already--in the time You've taken to describe his wishes to me!

PAGE.

The duke, I fear----

PRINCESS.

Again, the duke! What can The duke want here? What should a warrior want With my soft dreams of happiness? He should Have left him there, or sent him from his presence. Where is the man may not be treated thus?

But Carlos seems as little versed in love As in a woman's heart--he little knows What minutes are. But hark! I hear a step; Away, away!

[PAGE hastens out.

Where have I laid my lute?

I must not seem to wait for him. My song Shall be a signal to him.

56

SCENE VIII.

The PRINCESS, DON CARLOS.

The PRINCESS has thrown herself upon an ottoman, and plays.

CARLOS (rushes in; he recognizes the PRINCESS, and stands thunderstruck).

Gracious Heaven! Where am I?

PRINCESS (lets her lute fall, and meeting him) What? Prince Carlos! yes, in truth.

CARLOS.

Where am I? Senseless error; I have missed The right apartment.

PRINCESS.

With what dexterous skill

Carlos contrives to hit the very room Where ladies sit alone!

CARLOS.

Your pardon, princess!

I found--I found the antechamber open.

PRINCESS.

Can it be possible? I fastened it Myself; at least I thought so----

CARLOS.

Ay! you thought, You only thought so; rest assured you did not. You meant to lock it, that I well believe: But most assuredly it was not locked.

A lute's sweet sounds attracted me, some hand Touched it with skill; say, was it not a lute?

[Looking round inquiringly.

Yes, there it lies, and Heaven can bear me witness I love the lute to madness. I became

All ear, forgot myself in the sweet strain, And rushed into the chamber to behold The lovely eyes of the divine musician Who charmed me with the magic of her tones.

PRINCESS.

Innocent curiosity, no doubt!

But it was soon appeased, as I can prove.

[After a short silence, significantly. I must respect the modesty that has, To spare a woman's blushes, thus involved Itself in so much fiction.

CARLOS (with sincerity). Nay, I feel I but augment my deep embarrassment,

In vain attempt to extricate myself. Excuse me for a part I cannot play.

In this remote apartment, you perhaps Have sought a refuge from the world, to pour The inmost wishes of your secret heart Remote from man's distracting eye. By me, Unhappy that I am, your heavenly dreams Are all disturbed, and the atonement now Must be my speedy absence.

[Going.

PRINCESS (surprised and confused, but immediately recovering herself). Oh! that step

Were cruel, prince, indeed!

CARLOS.

Princess, I feel

What such a look in such a place imports: This virtuous embarrassment has claims To which my manhood never can be deaf.

Woe to the wretch whose boldness takes new fire From the pure blush of maiden modesty!

I am a coward when a woman trembles.

PRINCESS.

Is't possible?--such noble self-control

In one so young, and he a monarch's son! Now, prince, indeed you shall remain with me, It is my own request, and you must stay.

Near such high virtue, every maiden fear Takes wing at once; but your appearance here Disturbed me in a favorite air, and now Your penalty shall be to hear me sing it.

CARLOS (sits down near the PRINCESS, not without reluctance). A penalty delightful as the sin!

And sooth to say, the subject of the song Was so divine, again and yet again I'd gladly hear it.

PRINCESS

What! you heard it all?

Nay, that was too bad, prince. It was, I think, A song of love.

CARLOS.

And of successful love, If I mistake not--dear delicious theme From those most beauteous lips--but scarce so true, Methinks, as beautiful.

PRINCESS.

What! not so true?

Then do you doubt the tale?

CARLOS.

I almost doubt That Carlos and the Princess Eboli, When they discourse on such a theme as love, May not quite understand each other's hearts.

[The PRINCESS starts; he observes it, and continues with playful gallantry.

Who would believe those rosy-tinted cheeks Concealed a heart torn by the pangs of love. Is it within the range of wayward chance That the fair Princess Eboli should sigh Unheard--unanswered? Love is only known By him who hopelessly persists in love.

PRINCESS (with all her former vivacity). Hush! what a dreadful thought! this fate indeed Appears to follow you of all mankind, Especially to-day.

[Taking his hand with insinuating interest. You are not happy, Dear prince--you're sad! I know too well you suffer, And wherefore, prince? When with such loud appeal The world invites you to enjoy its bliss-- And nature on you pours her bounteous gifts, And spreads around you all life's sweetest joys. You, a great monarch's son, and more--far more-- E'en in your cradle with such gifts endowed As far eclipsed the splendor of your rank.

You, who in those strict courts where women rule, And pass, without appeal, unerring sentence On manly worth and honor, even there Find partial judges. You, who with a look Can prove victorious, and whose very coldness Kindles aflame; and who, when warmed with passion, Can make a paradise, and scatter round The bliss of heaven, the rapture of the gods. The man whom nature has adorned with gifts To render thousands happy, gifts which she Bestows on few--that such a man as this Should know what misery is! Thou, gracious Heaven, That gavest him all those blessings, why deny Him eyes to see the conquests he has made?

CARLOS

(who has been lost in absence of mind, suddenly recovers himself by the silence of the PRINCESS, and starts up). Charming! inimitable! Princess, sing That passage, pray, again.

PRINCESS

(looking at him with astonishment). Where, Carlos, were Your thoughts the while?

CARLOS (jumps up).

By heaven, you do remind me In proper time--I must away--and quickly.

PRINCESS

(Holding him back). Whither away?

CARLOS.

Into the open air.

Nay, do not hold me, princess, for I feel As though the world behind me were in flames.

PRINCESS (holding him forcibly back).

What troubles you? Whence comes these strange, these wild, Unnatural looks? Nay, answer me!

[CARLOS stops to reflect, she draws him to the sofa to her. Dear Carlos, You need repose, your blood is feverish.

Come, sit by me: dispel these gloomy fancies. Ask yourself frankly can your head explain The tumult of your heart--and if it can-- Say, can no knight be found in all the court, No lady, generous as fair, to cure you-- Rather, I should have said, to understand you? What, no one?

CARLOS (hastily, without thinking). If the Princess Eboli----

PRINCESS (delighted, quickly). Indeed!

CARLOS.

Would write a letter for me, a few words Of kindly intercession to my father;-- They say your influence is great.

PRINCESS.

Who says so? [Aside. Ha! was it jealousy that held thee mute!

CARLOS.

Perchance my story is already public. I had a sudden wish to visit Brabant Merely to win my spurs--no more. The king, Kind soul, is fearful the fatigues of war Might spoil my singing!

PRINCESS.

Prince, you play me false!

Confess that by this serpent subterfuge You would mislead me. Look me in the face, Deceitful one! and say would he whose thoughts Were only bent on warlike deeds--would he E'er stoop so low as, with deceitful hand, To steal fair ladies' ribbons when they drop, And then--your pardon! hoard them--with such care?

[With light action she opens his shirt frill, and seizes a ribbon which is there concealed.

CARLOS (drawing back with amazement). Nay, princess--that's too much--I am betrayed. You're not to be deceived. You are in league With spirits and with demons!

PRINCESS.

Are you then Surprised at this? What will you wager, Carlos But I recall some stories to your heart?

Nay, try it with me; ask whate'er you please, And if the triflings of my sportive fancy-- The sound half-uttered by the air absorbed-- The smile of joy checked by returning gloom-- If motions--looks from your own soul concealed Have not escaped my notice--judge if I Can err when thou wouldst have me understand thee?

CARLOS.

Why, this is boldly ventured; I accept The wager, princess. Then you undertake To make discoveries in my secret heart Unknown even to myself.

PRINCESS (displeased, but earnestly). Unknown to thee!

Reflect a moment, prince! Nay, look around; This boudoir's not the chamber of the queen, Where small deceits are practised with full license. You start, a sudden blush o'erspreads your face.

Who is so bold, so idle, you would ask, As to watch Carlos when he deems himself From scrutiny secure? Who was it, then, At the last palace-ball observed you leave The queen, your partner, standing in the dance, And join, with eager haste, the neighboring couple, To offer to the Princess Eboli The hand your royal partner should have claimed? An error, prince, his majesty himself, Who just then entered the apartment, noticed.

CARLOS

(with ironical smile). His majesty? And did he really so?

Of all men he should not have seen it.

PRINCESS.

Nor yet that other scene within the chapel, Which doubtless Carlos hath long since forgotten. Prostrate before the holy Virgin's image, You lay in prayer, when suddenly you heard-- 'Twas not your fault--a rustling from behind Of ladies' dresses. Then did Philip's son, A youth of hero courage, tremble like A heretic before the holy office.

On his pale lips died the half-uttered prayer. In ecstasy of passion, prince--the scene Was truly touching--for you seized the hand, The blessed Virgin's cold and holy hand, And showered your burning kisses on the marble.

CARLOS.

Princess, you wrong me: that was pure devotion!

PRINCESS.

Indeed! that's quite another thing. Perhaps It was the fear of losing, then, at cards, When you were seated with the queen and me, And you with dexterous skill purloined my glove.

[CARLOS starts surprised.

That prompted you to play it for a card?

CARLOS.

What words are these? O Heaven, what have I done?

PRINCESS.

Nothing I hope of which you need repent!

How pleasantly was I surprised to find Concealed within the glove a little note, Full of the warmest tenderest romance?

CARLOS (interrupting her suddenly). Mere poetry! no more. My fancy teems With idle bubbles oft, which break as soon As they arise--and this was one of them; So, prithee, let us talk of it no more.

PRINCESS (leaving him with astonishment, and regarding him for some time at a distance).

I am exhausted--all attempts are vain To hold this youth. He still eludes my grasp.

[Remains silent a few moments.

But stay! Perchance 'tis man's unbounded pride, That thus to add a zest to my delight.

Assumes a mask of timid diffidence. 'Tis so.

[She approaches the PRINCE again, and looks at him doubtingly. Explain yourself, prince, I entreat you.

For here I stand before a magic casket, Which all my keys are powerless to unlock.

CARLOS.

As I before you stand.

PRINCESS (leaves him suddenly, walks a few steps up and down in silence, apparently lost in deep thought. After a pause, gravely and solemnly).

Then thus at last-- I must resolve to speak, and Carlos, you Shall be my judge. Yours is a noble nature, You are a prince--a knight--a man of honor. I throw myself upon your heart--protect me Or if I'm lost beyond redemption's power, Give me your tears in pity for my fate.

[The PRINCE draws nearer.

A daring favorite of the king demands My hand--his name Ruy Gomez, Count of Silva, The king consents--the bargain has been struck, And I am sold already to his creature.

CARLOS (with evident emotion). Sold! you sold! Another bargain, then, Concluded by this royal southern trader!

PRINCESS.

No; but hear all--'tis not enough that I Am sacrificed to cold state policy, A snare is laid to entrap my innocence. Here is a letter will unmask the saint!

[CARLOS takes the paper, and without reading it listens with impatience to her recital.

Where Shall I find protection, prince? Till now My virtue was defended by my pride, At length----

CARLOS.

At length you yielded! Yielded? No. For God's sake say not so!

PRINCESS.

Yielded! to whom?

Poor piteous reasoning. Weak beyond contempt Your haughty minds, who hold a woman's favor, And love's pure joys, as wares to traffic for!

Love is the only treasure on the face Of this wide earth that knows no purchaser Besides itself--love has no price but love. It is the costly gem, beyond all price, Which I must freely give away, or—bury For ever unenjoyed--like that proud merchant Whom not the wealth of all the rich Rialto Could tempt--a great rebuke to kings! to save From the deep ocean waves his matchless pearl, Too proud to barter it beneath its worth!

CARLOS (aside).

Now, by great heaven, this woman's beautiful.

PRINCESS.

Call it caprice or pride, I ne'er will make Division of my joys. To him, alone, I choose as mine, I give up all forever. One only sacrifice I make; but that Shall be eternal. One true heart alone My love shall render happy: but that one I'll elevate to God. The keen delight Of mingling souls--the kiss--the swimming joys Of that delicious hour when lovers meet, The magic power of heavenly beauty--all Are sister colors of a single ray-- Leaves of one single blossom. Shall I tear One petal from this sweet, this lovely flower, With reckless hand, and mar its beauteous chalice? Shall I degrade the dignity of woman, The masterpiece of the Almighty's hand, To charm the evening of a reveller?

CARLOS.

Incredible! that in Madrid should dwell This matchless creature! and unknown to me Until this day.

PRINCESS.

Long since had I forsakenThis court--the world--and in some blest retreat Immured myself; but one tie binds me still Too firmly to existence. Perhaps--alas! 'Tis but a phantom--but 'tis dear to me. I love--but am not loved in turn.

CARLOS (full of ardor, going towards her). You are!

As true as God is throned in heaven! I swear You are--you are unspeakably beloved.

PRINCESS.

You swear it, you!--sure 'twas an angel's voice. Oh, if you swear it, Carlos, I'll believe it.

Then I am truly loved!

CARLOS (embracing her with tenderness). Bewitching maid, Thou creature worthy of idolatry I stand before thee now all eye, all ear, All rapture and delight. What eye hath seen thee-- Under yon heaven what eye could e'er have seen thee, And boast he never loved? What dost thou here In Philip's royal court! Thou beauteous angel! Here amid monks and all their princely train. This is no clime for such a lovely flower-- They fain would rifle all thy sweets--full well I know their hearts. But it shall never be-- Not whilst I draw life's breath. I fold thee thus Within my arms, and in these hands I'll bear thee E'en through a hell replete with mocking fiends. Let me thy guardian angel prove.

PRINCESS (with a countenance full of love). O Carlos!

How little have I known thee! and how richly With measureless reward thy heart repays The weighty task of--comprehending thee! [She takes his hand and is about to kiss it. CARLOS (drawing it back). Princess! What mean you?

PRINCESS (with tenderness and grace, looking at his hand attentively). Oh, this beauteous hand! How lovely 'tis, and rich! This hand has yet Two costly presents to bestow!--a crown-- And Carlos' heart:--and both these gifts perchance Upon one mortal!--both on one-- Oh, great And godlike gift-almost too much for one! How if you share the treasure, prince! A queen Knows naught of love--and she who truly loves Cares little for a crown! 'Twere better, prince, Then to divide the treasure--and at once--

What says my prince? Have you done so already? Have you in truth? And do I know the blest one?

CARLOS.

Thou shalt. I will unfold myself to thee, To thy unspotted innocence, dear maid, Thy pure, unblemished nature. In this court Thou art the worthiest--first--the only one To whom this soul has stood revealed.

Then, yes! I will not now conceal it--yes, I love!

PRINCESS.

Oh, cruel heart! Does this avowal prove So painful to thee? Must I first deserve Thy pity--ere I hope to win thy love?

CARLOS (starting). What say'st thou?

PRINCESS.

So to trifle with me, prince!

Indeed it was not well--and to deny The key----

CARLOS.

The key! the key! Oh yes, 'tis so! [After a dead silence.

I see it all too plainly! Gracious heaven!

[His knees totter, he leans against a chair, and covers his face with his hands. A long silence on both sides. The PRINCESS screams and falls.

PRINCESS.

Oh, horrible! What have I done!

CARLOS.

Hurled down

So far from all my heavenly joys! 'Tis dreadful!

PRINCESS (hiding her face in the cushion). Oh, God! What have I said?

CARLOS (kneeling before her). I am not guilty.

My passion--an unfortunate mistake-- By heaven, I am not guilty----

PRINCESS (pushing him from her).

Out of my sight, For heaven's sake!

CARLOS.

No, I will not leave thee thus.

In this dread anguish leave thee---- PRINCESS (pushing him forcibly away).

Oh, in pity-- For mercy's sake, away--out of my sight! Wouldst thou destroy me? How I hate thy presence! [CARLOS going.

65

Give, give me back the letter and the key. Where is the other letter?

CARLOS.

The other letter?

PRINCESS.

That from the king, to me----

CARLOS (terrified).

From whom?

PRINCESS.

The one I just now gave you.

CARLOS.

From the king! To you!

PRINCESS.

Oh, heavens, how dreadfully have I Involved myself! The letter, sir! I must Have it again.

CARLOS.

The letter from the king! To you!

PRINCESS.

The letter! give it, I implore you By all that's sacred! give it.

CARLOS.

What, the letter That will unmask the saint! Is this the letter?

PRINCESS.

Now I'm undone! Quick, give it me----

CARLOS.

The letter----

PRINCESS (wringing her hands in despair). What have I done? O dreadful, dire imprudence!

CARLOS.

This letter comes, then, from the king! Princess, That changes all indeed, and quickly, too.

This letter is beyond all value--priceless!

All Philip's crowns are worthless, and too poor To win it from my hands. I'll keep this letter.

PRINCESS (throwing herself prostrate before him as he is going). Almighty Heaven! then I am lost forever.

[Exit CARLOS.

SCENE IX.

The PRINCESS alone.

She seems overcome with surprise, and is confounded. After CARLOS' departure she hastens to call him back.

PRINCESS.

Prince, but one word! Prince, hear me. He is gone. And this, too, I am doomed to bear--his scorn!

And I am left in lonely wretchedness, Rejected and despised!

[Sinks down upon a chair. After a pause And yet not so; I'm but displaced--supplanted by some wanton. He loves! of that no longer doubt is left; He has himself confessed it--but my rival-- Who can she be? Happy, thrice happy one! This much stands clear: he loves where he should not. He dreads discovery, and from the king He hides his guilty passion! Why from him Who would so gladly hail it? Or, is it not The father that he dreads so in the parent?

When the king's wanton purpose was disclosed, His features glowed with triumph, boundless joy Flashed in his eyes, his rigid virtue fled; Why was it mute in such a cause as this? Why should he triumph? What hath he to gain If Philip to his queen---- [She stops suddenly, as if struck by a thought, then drawing hastily from her bosom the ribbon which she had taken from CARLOS, she seems to recognize it. Fool that I am! At length 'tis plain. Where have my senses been? My eyes are opened now. They loved each other Long before Philip wooed her, and the prince Ne'er saw me but with her! She, she alone Was in his thoughts when I believed myself The object of his true and boundless love.

O matchless error! and have I betrayed My weakness to her?

[Pauses.

Should his love prove hopeless?

Who can believe it? Would a hopeless love Persist in such a struggle? Called to revel In joys for which a monarch sighs in vain! A hopeless love makes no such sacrifice. What fire was in his kiss! How tenderly He pressed my bosom to his beating heart! Well nigh the trial had proved dangerous To his romantic, unrequited passion! With joy he seized the key he fondly thought The queen had sent:--in this gigantic stride Of love he puts full credence--and he comes-- In very truth comes here--and so imputes To Philip's wife a deed so madly rash.

And would he so, had love not made him bold? 'Tis clear as day--his suit is heard--she loves! By heaven, this saintly creature burns with passion; How subtle, too, she is! With fear I trembled Before this lofty paragon of virtue!

She towered beside me, an exalted being, And in her beams I felt myself eclipsed; I envied her the lovely, cloudless calm, That kept her soul from earthly tumults free. And was this soft serenity but show?

Would she at both feasts revel, holding up Her virtue's godlike splendor to our gaze, And riot in the secret joys of vice?

And shall the false dissembler cozen thus, And win a safe immunity from this That no avenger comes? By heavens she shall not! I once adored her,--that demands revenge:-- The king shall know her treachery--the king!

[After a pause.

'Tis the sure way to win the monarch's ear! [Exit.

SCENE X.

A chamber in the royal palace.

DUKE OF ALVA, FATHER DOMINGO.

DOMINGO.

Something to tell me!

ALVA.

Ay! a thing of moment, Of which I made discovery to-day, And I would have your judgment on it.

DOMINGO.

How!

Discovery! To what do you allude?

ALVA.

Prince Carlos and myself this morning met In the queen's antechamber. I received An insult from him--we were both in heat-- The strife grew loud--and we had drawn our swords. Alarmed, from her apartments rushed the queen.

She stepped between us,--with commanding eye Of conscious power, she looked upon the prince. 'Twas but a single glance,--but his arm dropped, He fell upon my bosom--gave me then

A warm embrace, and vanished. DOMINGO (after a pause).

This seems strange.

It brings a something to my mind, my lord!

And thoughts like these I own have often sprung Within my breast; but I avoid such fancies-- To no one have I e'er confided them.

There are such things as double-edged swords And untrue friends,--I fear them both.

'Tis hard to judge among mankind, but still more hard To know them thoroughly. Words slipped at random Are confidants offended--therefore I Buried my secret in my breast, till time Should drag it forth to light. 'Tis dangerous To render certain services to kings.

They are the bolts, which if they miss the mark, Recoil upon the archer! I could swear Upon the sacrament to what I saw.

Yet one eye-witness--one word overheard-- A scrap of paper--would weigh heavier far Than my most strong conviction! Cursed fate That we are here in Spain!

ALVA.

And why in Spain?

DOMINGO.

There is a chance in every court but this For passion to forget itself, and fall.

Here it is warned by ever-wakeful laws.

Our Spanish queens would find it hard to sin-- And only there do they meet obstacles, Where best 'twould serve our purpose to surprise them.

ALVA.

But listen further: Carlos had to-day An audience of the king; the interview Lasted an hour, and earnestly he sought The government of Flanders for himself. Loudly he begged, and fervently. I heard him In the adjoining cabinet. His eyes Were red with tears when I encountered him. At noon he wore a look of lofty triumph, And vowed his joy at the king's choice of me.

He thanked the king. "Matters are changed," he said, "And things go better now." He's no dissembler: How shall I reconcile such contradictions?

The prince exults to see himself rejected, And I receive a favor from the king With marks of anger! What must I believe? In truth this new-born dignity doth sound Much more like banishment than royal favor!

DOMINGO.

And is it come to this at last? to this? And has one moment crumbled into dust What cost us years to build? And you so calm, So perfectly at ease! Know you this youth? Do you foresee the fate we may expect Should he attain to power? The prince! No foe Am I of his. Far other cares than these Gnaw at my rest--cares for the throne--for God, And for his holy church! The royal prince-- (I know him, I can penetrate his soul), Has formed a horrible design, Toledo! The wild design--to make himself the regent, And set aside our pure and sacred faith. His bosom glows with some new-fangled virtue, Which, proud and self-sufficient, scorns to rest For strength on any creed. He dares to think! His brain is all on fire with wild chimeras; He reverences the people! And is this A man to be our king?

ALVA.

Fantastic dreams!

No more. A boy's ambition, too, perchance To play some lofty part! What can he less?

These thoughts will vanish when he's called to rule.

DOMINGO.

I doubt it! Of his freedom he is proud, And scorns those strict restraints all men must bear Who hope to govern others. Would he suit Our throne? His bold gigantic mind Would burst the barriers of our policy. In vain I sought to enervate his soul In the loose joys of this voluptuous age. He stood the trial. Fearful is the spirit That rules this youth; and Philip soon will see His sixtieth year.

ALVA.

Your vision stretches far!

DOMINGO.

He and the queen are both alike in this. Already works, concealed in either breast, The poisonous wish for change and innovation. Give it but way, 'twill quickly reach the throne. I know this Valois! We may tremble for The secret vengeance of this quiet foe If Philip's weakness hearken to her voice! Fortune so far hath smiled upon us. Now We must anticipate the foe, and both Shall fall together in one fatal snare.

Let but a hint of such a thing be dropped Before the king, proved or unproved, it reeks not! Our point is gained if he but waver. We Ourselves have not a doubt; and once convinced, 'Tis easy to convince another's mind. Be sure we shall discover more if we Start with the faith that more remains concealed.

ALVA.

But soft! A vital question! Who is he Will undertake the task to tell the king?

DOMINGO.

Nor you, nor I! Now shall you learn, what long My busy spirit, full of its design, Has been at work with, to achieve its ends. Still is there wanting to complete our league A third important personage. The king Loves the young Princess Eboli--and I Foster this passion for my own designs.

I am his go-between. She shall be schooled Into our plot. If my plan fail me not, In this young lady shall a close ally-- A very queen, bloom for us. She herself Asked me, but now, to meet her in this chamber. I'm full of hope. And in one little night A Spanish maid may blast this Valois lily.

ALVA.

What do you say! Can I have heard aright? By Heaven! I'm all amazement. Compass this, And I'll bow down to thee, Dominican!

The day's our own.

DOMINGO.

Soft! Some one comes: 'tis she-- 'Tis she herself!

ALVA.

I'm in the adjoining room If you should----

DOMINGO.

Be it so: I'll call you in. [Exit ALVA.

SCENE XI.

PRINCESS, DOMINGO. DOMINGO.

At your command, princess.

PRINCESS.

We are perhaps Not quite alone?

[Looking inquisitively after the DUKE. You have, as I observe, A witness still by you.

DOMINGO.

How?

PRINCESS.

Who was he, That left your side but now?

DOMINGO.

It was Duke ALVA.

Most gracious princess, he requests you will Admit him to an audience after me.

PRINCESS.

Duke Alva! How? What can he want with me? You can, perhaps, inform me?

DOMINGO.

I?--and that Before I learn to what important chance I owe the favor, long denied, to stand Before the Princess Eboli once more?

[Pauses awaiting her answer.

Has any circumstance occurred at last To favor the king's wishes? Have my hopes Been not in vain, that more deliberate thought Would reconcile you to an offer which Caprice alone and waywardness could spurn? I seek your presence full of expectation----

PRINCESS.

Was my last answer to the king conveyed?

DOMINGO.

I have delayed to inflict this mortal wound. There still is time, it rests with you, princess, To mitigate its rigor.

PRINCESS.

Tell the king That I expect him.

DOMINGO.

May I, lovely princess, Indeed accept this as your true reply?

PRINCESS.

I do not jest. By heaven, you make me tremble What have I done to make e'en you grow pale?

DOMINGO.

Nay, lady, this surprise--so sudden--I Can scarcely comprehend it.

PRINCESS.

Reverend sir!

You shall not comprehend it. Not for all The world would I you comprehended it. Enough for you it is so--spare yourself The trouble to investigate in thought,

Whose eloquence hath wrought this wondrous change. But for your comfort let me add, you have No hand in this misdeed,--nor has the church. Although you've proved that cases might arise Wherein the church, to gain some noble end, Might use the persons of her youthful daughters! Such reasonings move not me; such motives, pure, Right reverend sir, are far too high for me.

DOMINGO.

When they become superfluous, your grace, I willingly retract them.

PRINCESS.

Seek the king, And ask him as from me, that he will not Mistake me in this business. What I have been That am I still. 'Tis but the course of things Has changed. When I in anger spurned his suit, I deemed him truly happy in possessing

Earth's fairest queen. I thought his faithful wife Deserved my sacrifice. I thought so then, But now I'm undeceived.

DOMINGO.

Princess, go on!

I hear it all--we understand each other.

PRINCESS.

Enough. She is found out. I will not spare her. The hypocrite's unmasked!--She has deceived The king, all Spain, and me. She loves, I know She loves! I can bring proofs that will make you tremble. The king has been deceived--but he shall not, By heaven, go unrevenged! The saintly mask Of pure and superhuman self-denial I'll tear from her deceitful brow, that all

May see the forehead of the shameless sinner. 'Twill cost me dear, but here my triumph lies, That it will cost her infinitely more.

DOMINGO.

Now all is ripe, let me call in the duke. [Goes out.

PRINCESS (astonished). What means all this?

SCENE XII.

The PRINCESS, DUKE ALVA, DOMINGO.

DOMINGO (leading the DUKE in). Our tidings, good my lord,

Come somewhat late. The Princess Eboli Reveals to us a secret we had meant Ourselves to impart to her.

ALVA.

My visit, then,

Will not so much surprise her, but I never Trust my own eyes in these discoveries.

They need a woman's more discerning glance.

PRINCESS.

Discoveries! How mean you?

DOMINGO.

Would we knew

What place and fitter season you----

PRINCESS.

Just So!

To-morrow noon I will expect you both. Reasons I have why this clandestine guilt Should from the king no longer be concealed.

ALVA.

'Tis this that brings us here. The king must know it. And he shall hear the news from you, princess,

From you alone:--for to what tongue would he Afford such ready credence as to yours, Friend and companion ever of his spouse?

DOMINGO.

As yours, who more than any one at will Can o'er him exercise supreme command.

ALVA.

I am the prince's open enemy.

DOMINGO.

And that is what the world believes of me. The Princess Eboli's above suspicion.

We are compelled to silence, but your duty, The duty of your office, calls on you

To speak. The king shall not escape our hands. Let your hints rouse him, we'll complete the work.

ALVA.

It must be done at once, without delay; Each moment now is precious. In an hour The order may arrive for my departure.

DOMINGO (after a short pause, turns to the PRINCESS). Cannot some letters be discovered? Truly, An intercepted letter from the prince Would work with rare effect. Ay! let me see-- Is it not so? You sleep, princess, I think, In the same chamber with her majesty?

PRINCESS.

The next to hers. But of what use is that?

DOMINGO.

Oh, for some skill in locks! Have you observed Where she is wont to keep her casket key?

PRINCESS (in thought).

Yes, that might lead to something; yes, I think The key is to be found.

DOMINGO.

Letters, you know, Need messengers. Her retinue is large; Who do you think could put us on the scent? Gold can do much.

ALVA.

Can no one tell us whether The prince has any trusty confidant?

DOMINGO.

Not one; in all Madrid not one.

ALVA.

That's strange!

DOMINGO.

Rely on me in this. He holds in scorn The universal court. I have my proofs.

ALVA.

Stay! It occurs to me, as I was leaving The queen's apartments, I beheld the prince In private conference with a page of hers.

PRINCESS (suddenly interrupting).

O no! that must have been of something else.

DOMINGO.

Could we not ascertain the fact? It seems Suspicious.

[To the DUKE.

Did you know the page, my lord!

PRINCESS.

Some trifle; what else could it be?

Enough, I'm sure of that. So we shall meet again Before I see the king; and by that time

We may discover much. DOMINGO (leading her aside).

What of the king?

Say, may he hope? May I assure him so? And the entrancing hour which shall fulfil His fond desires, what shall I say of that?

PRINCESS.

In a few days I will feign sickness, and Shall be excused from waiting on the queen. Such is, you know, the custom of the court, And I may then remain in my apartment.

DOMINGO.

'Tis well devised! Now the great game is won, And we may bid defiance to all queens!

PRINCESS.

Hark! I am called. I must attend the queen, So fare you well.

[Exit.

SCENE XIII.

ALVA and DOMINGO.

DOMINGO (after a pause, during which he has watched the PRINCESS). My lord! these roses, and-- Your battles----

ALVA.

And your god!--why, even so Thus we'll await the lightning that will scathe us! [Exeunt.

SCENE XIV.

A Carthusian Convent.

DON CARLOS and the PRIOR.

CARLOS (to the PRIOR, as he comes in). Been here already? I am sorry for it.

PRIOR.

Yes, thrice since morning. 'Tis about an hour Since he went hence.

CARLOS.

But he will sure return.

Has he not left some message?

PRIOR.

Yes; he promised

To come again at noon.

CARLOS (going to a window, and looking round the country). Your convent lies

Far from the public road. Yonder are seen The turrets of Madrid--just so--and there The Mansanares flows. The scenery is Exactly to my wish, and all around

Is calm and still as secrecy itself.

PRIOR.

Or as the entrance to another world.

CARLOS.

Most worthy sir, to your fidelity And honor, have I now intrusted all I hold most dear and sacred in the world. No mortal man must know, or even suspect, With whom I here hold secret assignation.

Most weighty reasons prompt me to deny, To all the world, the friend whom I expect, Therefore I choose this convent. Are we safe From traitors and surprise? You recollect What you have sworn.

PRIOR.

Good sir, rely on us.

A king's suspicion cannot pierce the grave, And curious ears haunts only those resorts Where wealth and passion dwell--but from these walls The world's forever banished.

CARLOS.

You may think, Perhaps, beneath this seeming fear and caution There lies a guilty conscience?

PRIOR.

I think nothing.

CARLOS.

If you imagine this, most holy father, You err--indeed you err. My secret shuns The sight of man--but not the eye of God.

PRIOR.

Such things concern us little. This retreat To guilt, and innocence alike, is open, And whether thy designs be good or ill, Thy purpose criminal or virtuous,--that We leave to thee to settle with thy heart.

CARLOS (with warmth).

Our purpose never can disgrace your God. 'Tis his own noblest work. To you indeed, I may reveal it.

PRIOR.

To what end, I pray?

Forego, dear prince, this needless explanation. The world and all its troubles have been long Shut from my thoughts--in preparation for My last long journey. Why recall them to me For the brief space that must precede my death? 'Tis little for salvation that we need-- But the bell rings, and summons me to prayer.

[Exit PRIOR.

SCENE XV.

DON CARLOS; the MARQUIS POSA enters.

CARLOS.

At length once more,--at length----

MARQUIS.

Oh, what a trial For the impatience of a friend! The sun Has risen twice--twice set--since Carlos' fate Has been resolved, and am I only now To learn it: speak,--you're reconciled!

CARLOS.

With whom?

MARQUIS.

The king! And Flanders, too,--its fate is settled!

CARLOS.

The duke sets out to-morrow. That is fixed.

MARQUIS.

That cannot be--it is not surely so.

Can all Madrid be so deceived? 'Tis said You had a private audience, and the king----

CARLOS.

Remained inflexible, and we are now Divided more than ever.

MARQUIS.

Do you go To Flanders?

CARLOS.

No!

MARQUIS.

Alas! my blighted hopes!

CARLOS.

Of this hereafter. Oh, Roderigo! since We parted last, what have I not endured? But first thy counsel? I must speak with her!

MARQUIS.

Your mother? No! But wherefore?

CARLOS.

I have hopes-- But you turn pale! Be calm--I should be happy. And I shall be so: but of this anon-- Advise me now, how I may speak with her.

MARQUIS.

What mean you? What new feverish dream is this?

CARLOS.

By the great God of wonders 'tis no dream! 'Tis truth, reality----

[Taking out the KING's letter to the PRINCESS EBOLI.

Contained in this Important paper--yes, the queen is free,-- Free before men and in the eyes of heaven; There read, and cease to wonder at my words.

MARQUIS (opening the letter).

What do I here behold? The king's own hand!

[After he has read it. To whom addressed?

CARLOS.

To Princess Eboli.

Two days ago, a page who serves the queen, Brought me, from unknown hands, a key and letter, Which said that in the left wing of the palace, Where the queen lodges, lay a cabinet,-- That there a lady whom I long had loved Awaited me. I straight obeyed the summons.

MARQUIS.

Fool! madman! you obeyed it----

CARLOS.

Not that I

The writing knew; but there was only one Such woman, who could think herself adored By Carlos. With delight intoxicate I hastened to the spot. A heavenly song, Re-echoing from the innermost apartment, Served me for guide. I reached the cabinet-- I entered and beheld-- conceive my wonder!

MARQUIS.

I guess it all----

CARLOS.

I had been lost forever, But that I fell into an angel's hands!

She, hapless chance, by my imprudent looks, Deceived, had yielded to the sweet delusion And deemed herself the idol of my soul.

Moved by the silent anguish of my breast, With thoughtless generosity, her heart Nobly determined to return my love; Deeming respectful fear had caused my silence, She dared to speak, and all her lovely soul Laid bare before me.

MARQUIS.

And with calm composure, You tell this tale! The Princess Eboli Saw through your heart; and doubtless she has pierced The inmost secret of your hidden love.

You've wronged her deeply, and she rules the king.

CARLOS (confidently). But she is virtuous!

MARQUIS.

She may be so From love's mere selfishness. But much I fear Such virtue--well I know it: know how little It hath the power to soar to that ideal, Which, first conceived in sweet and stately grace, From the pure soul's maternal soil, puts forth Spontaneous shoots, nor asks the gardener's aid To nurse its lavish blossoms into life.

'Tis but a foreign plant, with labor reared, And warmth that poorly imitates the south, In a cold soil and an unfriendly clime.

Call it what name you will--or education, Or principle, or artificial virtue Won from the heat of youth by art and cunning, In conflicts manifold--all noted down With scrupulous reckoning to that heaven's account, Which is its aim, and will requite its pains.

Ask your own heart! Can she forgive the queen That you should scorn her dearly-purchased virtue, To pine in hopeless love for Philip's wife.

CARLOS.

Knowest thou the princess, then, so well?

MARQUIS.

Not I-- I've scarcely seen her twice. And yet thus much I may remark. To me she still appears To shun alone the nakedness of vice, Too weakly proud of her imagined virtue. And then I mark the queen. How different, Carlos, Is everything that I behold in her!

In native dignity, serene and calm, Wearing a careless cheerfulness--unschooled In all the trained restraints of conduct, far Removed from boldness and timidity, With firm, heroic step, she walks along The narrow middle path of rectitude, Unconscious of the worship she compels, Where she of self-approval never dreamed. Say, does my Carlos in this mirror trace The features of his Eboli? The princess Was constant while she loved; love was the price, The understood condition of her virtue.

You failed to pay that price--'twill therefore fall.

CARLOS (with warmth).

No, no!

[Hastily pacing the apartment. I tell thee, no! And, Roderigo, Ill it becomes thee thus to rob thy Carlos Of his high trust in human excellence, His chief, his dearest joy!

MARQUIS.

Deserve I this?

Friend of my soul, this would I never do-- By heaven I would not. Oh, this Eboli!

She were an angel to me, and before Her glory would I bend me prostrate down, In reverence deep as thine, if she were not The mistress of thy secret.

CARLOS.

See how vain, How idle are thy fears! What proofs has she That will not stamp her maiden brow with shame? Say, will she purchase with her own dishonor The wretched satisfaction of revenge?

MARQUIS.

Ay! to recall a blush, full many a one Has doomed herself to infamy.

CARLOS (with increased vehemence).

Nay, that Is far too harsh--and cruel! She is proud And noble; well I know her, and fear nothing. Vain are your efforts to alarm my hopes.

I must speak to my mother.

MARQUIS.

Now? for what?

CARLOS.

Because I've nothing more to care for now. And I must know my fate. Only contrive That I may speak with her.

MARQUIS.

And wilt thou show This letter to her?

CARLOS.

Question me no more, But quickly find the means that I may see her.

MARQUIS (significantly).

Didst thou not tell me that thou lov'st thy mother? And wouldst thou really show this letter to her?

[CARLOS fixes his eyes on the ground, and remains silent. I read a something, Carlos, in thy looks

Unknown to me before. Thou turn'st thine eyes Away from me. Then it is true, and have I Judged thee aright? Here, let me see that paper.

[CARLOS gives him the letter, and the MARQUIS tears it.

CARLOS.

What! art thou mad?

[Moderating his warmth. In truth--I must confess it, That letter was of deepest moment to me.

MARQUIS.

So it appeared: on that account I tore it.

[The MARQUIS casts a penetrating look on the PRINCE, who surveys him with doubt and surprise. A long silence.

Now speak to me with candor, Carlos. What Have desecrations of the royal bed To do with thee--thy love? Dost thou fear Philip? How are a husband's violated duties

Allied with thee and thy audacious hopes?

Has he sinned there, where thou hast placed thy love? Now then, in truth, I learn to comprehend thee-- How ill till now I've understood thy love!

CARLOS.

What dost thou think, Roderigo?

MARQUIS.

Oh, I feel From what it is that I must wean myself. Once it was otherwise! Yes, once thy soul Was bounteous, rich, and warm, and there was room For a whole world in thy expanded heart. Those feelings are extinct--all swallowed up In one poor, petty, selfish passion. Now

Thy heart is withered, dead! No tears last thou For the unhappy fate of wretched Flanders-- No, not another tear. Oh, Carlos! See How poor, how beggarly, thou hast become, Since all thy love has centered in thyself!

CARLOS

(flings himself into a chair. After a pause, with scarcely suppressed tears). Too well I know thou lovest me no more!

MARQUIS.

Not so, my Carlos. Well I understand This fiery passion: 'tis the misdirection Of feelings pure and noble in themselves.

The queen belonged to thee: the king, thy father, Despoiled thee of her--yet till now thou hast Been modestly distrustful of thy claims.

Philip, perhaps, was worthy of her! Thou Scarce dared to breathe his sentence in a whisper-- This letter has resolved thy doubts, and proved Thou art the worthier man. With haughty joy Thou saw'st before thee rise the doom that waits On tyranny convicted of a theft, But thou wert proud to be the injured one: Wrongs undeserved great souls can calmly suffer, Yet here thy fancy played thee false: thy pride Was touched with satisfaction, and thy heart Allowed itself to hope: I plainly saw This time, at least, thou didst not know thyself.

CARLOS (with emotion).

Thou'rt wrong, Roderigo; for my thoughts were far Less noble than thy goodness would persuade me.

MARQUIS.

And am I then e'en here so little known? See, Carlos, when thou errest, 'tis my way, Amid a hundred virtues, still to find That one to which I may impute thy fall. Now, then, we understand each other better, And thou shalt have an audience of the queen.

CARLOS (falling on his neck). Oh, how I blush beside thee!

MARQUIS.

Take my word, And leave the rest to me. A wild, bold thought, A happy thought is dawning in my mind; And thou shalt hear it from a fairer mouth, I hasten to the queen. Perhaps to-morrow Thy wish may be achieved. Till then, my Carlos, Forget not this--"That a design conceived Of lofty reason, which involves the fate, The sufferings of mankind, though it be baffled Ten thousand times, should never be abandoned." Dost hear? Remember Flanders.

CARLOS.

Yes! all, all That thou and virtue bid me not forget.

MARQUIS

(going to a window).

The time is up--I hear thy suite approaching.

[They embrace.

Crown prince again, and the vassal.

CARLOS.

Dost thou go Straight to Madrid?

MARQUIS.

Yes, straight.

CARLOS.

Hold! one word more.

How nearly it escaped me! Yet 'twas news Of deep importance. "Every letter now Sent to Brabant is opened by the king!" So be upon thy guard. The royal post Has secret orders.

MARQUIS.

How have you learned this?

CARLOS.

Don Raymond Taxis is my trusty friend.

MARQUIS (after a pause).

Well! then they may be sent through Germany. [Exeunt on different sides.

ACT III.

SCENE I.

The king's bedchamber. On the toilet two burning lights. In the background several pages asleep resting on their knees. The KING, in half undress, stands before the table, with one arm bent over the chair, in a reflecting posture. Before him is a medallion and papers.

KING.

Of a warm fancy she has ever been! Who can deny it? I could never love her,

Yet has she never seemed to miss my love. And so 'tis plain--she's false!

[Makes a movement which brings him to himself. He looks round with surprise.

Where have I been?

Is no one watching here, then, save the king? The light's burnt out, and yet it is not day.

I must forego my slumbers for to-night. Take it, kind nature, for enjoyed! No time

Have monarchs to retrieve the nights they lose. I'm now awake, and day it shall be.

[He puts out the candles, and draws aside the window-curtain. He observes the sleeping pages--remains for some time standing before them--then rings a bell.

All Asleep within the antechamber, too?

SCENE II.

The KING, COUNT LERMA.

LERMA (surprised at seeing the KING). Does not your majesty feel well?

KING.

The left Pavilion of the palace was in flames: Did you not hear the alarum?

LERMA.

No, my liege.

KING.

No! What? And did I only dream it then?

'Twas surely real! Does not the queen sleep there?

LERMA.

She does, your majesty.

KING.

This dream affrights me!

In future let the guards be doubled there As soon as it grows dark. Dost hear? And yet Let it be done in secret. I would not---- Why do you gaze on me?

LERMA.

Your bloodshot eyes, I mark, that beg repose. Dare I remind My liege of an inestimable life, And of your subjects, who with pale dismay Would in such features read of restless nights? But two brief hours of morning sleep would----

KING

(with troubled look).

Shall I find sleep within the Escurial?

Let the king sleep, and he may lose his crown, The husband, his wife's heart. But no! not so; This is but slander. Was it not a woman Whispered the crime to me? Woman, thy name Is calumny? The deed I'll hold unproved, Until a man confirms the fatal truth!

[To the pages, who in the meanwhile have awaked. Summon Duke Alva!

[Pages go.

Count, come nearer to me.

[Fixes a searching look on the COUNT. Is all this true? Oh for omniscience now,

Though but so long as a man's pulse might beat. Is it true? Upon your oath! Am I deceived?

LERMA.

My great, my best of kings! KING (drawing back).

King! naught but king!

And king again! No better answer than Mere hollow echo! When I strike this rock For water, to assuage my burning thirst, It gives me molten gold.

LERMA.

What true, my liege?

KING.

Oh, nothing, nothing! Leave me! Get thee gone!

[The COUNT going, the KING calls him back again. Say, are you married? and are you a father?

LERMA.

I am, your majesty.

KING.

What! married—yet You dare to watch a night here with your king! Your hair is gray, and yet you do not blush To think your wife is honest. Get thee home; You'll find her locked, this moment, in your son's Incestuous embrace. Believe your king.

Now go; you stand amazed; you stare at me With searching eye, because of my gray hairs. Unhappy man, reflect. Queens never taint Their virtue thus: doubt it, and you shall die!

LERMA (with warmth).

Who dare do so? In all my monarch's realms Who has the daring hardihood to breathe Suspicion on her angel purity?

To slander thus the best of queens----

KING.

The best!

The best, from you, too! She has ardent friends, I find, around. It must have cost her much-- More than methinks she could afford to give.

You are dismissed; now send the duke to me.

LERMA.

I hear him in the antechamber.

[Going.

KING (with a milder tone). Count, What you observed is very true. My head Burns with the fever of this sleepless night! What I have uttered in this waking dream, Mark you, forget! I am your gracious king!

[Presents his hand to kiss. Exit LERMA, opening the door at the same time to DUKE ALVA.

SCENE III.

The KING and DUKE ALVA.

ALVA (approaching the KING with an air of doubt). This unexpected order, at so strange

An hour!

[Starts on looking closer at the KING. And then those looks!

KING (has seated himself, and taken hold of the medallion on the table. Looks at the DUKE for some time in silence).

Is it true I have no faithful servant!

ALVA.

How?

KING.

A blow Aimed at my life in its most vital part!

Full well 'twas known, yet no one warned me of it.

ALVA (with a look of astonishment). A blow aimed at your majesty! and yet Escape your Alva's eye?

KING

(showing him letters). Know you this writing?

ALVA.

It is the prince's hand.

KING (a pause--watches the DUKE closely). Do you suspect Then nothing? Often have you cautioned me Gainst his ambition. Was there nothing more Than his ambition should have made me tremble?

ALVA.

Ambition is a word of largest import, And much it may comprise.

KING.

And had you naught Of special purport to disclose? ALVA (after a pause, mysteriously). Your majesty

Hath given the kingdom's welfare to my charge: On this my inmost, secret thoughts are bent, And my best vigilance. Beyond this charge What I may think, suspect, or know belongs To me alone. These are the sacred treasures Which not the vassal only, but the slave, The very slave, may from a king withhold. Not all that to my mind seems plain is yet Mature enough to meet the monarch's ear.

Would he be answered--then must I implore He will not question as a king.

KING

(handing the letters). Read these.

ALVA (reads them, and turns to the KING with a look of terror). Who was the madman placed these fatal papers

In my king's bands?

KING.

You know, then, who is meant?

No name you see is mentioned in the paper.

ALVA (stepping back confused). I was too hasty!

KING.

But you know!

ALVA (after some consideration). 'Tis spoken!

The king commands,--I dare not now conceal. I'll not deny it--I do know the person.

KING (starting up in violent emotion). God of revenge! inspire me to invent Some new, unheard-of torture! Is their crime So clear, so plain, so public to the world, That without e'en the trouble of inquiry The veriest hint suffices to reveal it? This is too much! I did not dream of this! I am the last of all, then, to discern it-- The last in all my realm?

ALVA

(Throwing himself at the KING'S feet). Yes, I confess My guilt, most gracious monarch. I'm ashamed A coward prudence should have tied my tongue When truth, and justice, and my sovereign's honor Urged me to speak. But since all else are silent And since the magic spell of beauty binds All other tongues, I dare to give it voice; Though well I know a son's warm protestations, A wife's seductive charms and winning tears---- KING (suddenly with warmth). Rise, Alva! thou hast now my royal promise; Rise, and speak fearlessly!

ALVA (rising). Your majesty, Perchance, may bear in your remembrance still What happened in the garden at Aranjuez. You found the queen deserted by her ladies, With looks confused--alone, within a bower,--

KING.

Proceed. What further have I yet to hear?

ALVA.

The Marchioness of Mondecar was banished Because she boldly sacrificed herself

To save the queen! It has been since discovered She did no more than she had been commanded. Prince Carlos had been there.

KING (starting).

The prince! What more?

ALVA.

Upon the ground the footsteps of a man Were traced, till finally they disappeared Close to a grotto, leftward of the bower, Where lay a handkerchief the prince had dropped. This wakened our suspicions. But besides, The gardener met the prince upon the spot,-- Just at the time, as near as we can guess, Your majesty appeared within the walk.

KING (recovering from gloomy thought). And yet she wept when I but seemed to doubt!

She made me blush before the assembled court, Blush to my very self! By heaven! I stood In presence of her virtue, like a culprit.

[A long and deep silence. He sits down and hides his face. Yes, Alva, you are right! All this may lead To something dreadful--leave me for a moment----

ALVA.

But, gracious sire, all this is not enough----

KING

(snatching up the papers).

Nor this, nor this?--nor all the harmony Of these most damning proofs? 'Tis clear as day-- I knew it long ago--their heinous guilt Began when first I took her from your hands, Here in Madrid. I think I see her now, With look of horror, pale as midnight ghost, Fixing her eyes upon my hoary hair!

'Twas then the treacherous game began!

ALVA.

The prince, In welcoming a mother--lost his bride!

Long had they nursed a mutual passion, long Each other's ardent feelings understood, Which her new state forbade her to indulge. The fear which still attends love's first avowal Was long subdued. Seduction, bolder grown, Spoke in those forms of easy confidence Which recollections of the past allowed.

Allied by harmony of souls and years, And now by similar restraints provoked, They readily obeyed their wild desires.

Reasons of state opposed their early union-- But can it, sire, be thought she ever gave To the state council such authority?

That she subdued the passion of her soul To scrutinize with more attentive eye The election of the cabinet. Her heart Was bent on love, and won a diadem.

KING (offended, and with bitterness). You are a nice observer, duke, and I Admire your eloquence. I thank you truly.

[Rising coldly and haughtily.

But you are right. The queen has deeply erred In keeping from me letters of such import, And in concealing the intrusive visit The prince paid in the garden:--from a false Mistaken honor she has deeply erred And I shall question further. [Ringing the bell. Who waits now Within the antechamber? You, Duke Alva, I need no longer. Go.

ALVA.

And has my zeal A second time displeased your majesty?

KING

(to a page who enters).

Summon Domingo. Duke, I pardon you For having made me tremble for a moment, With secret apprehension, lest yourself Might fall a victim to a foul misdeed.

[Exit ALVA.

SCENE IV.

The KING, DOMINGO.

KING walks up and down the room to collect his thoughts.

DOMINGO (after contemplating the KING for some time with a respectful silence).

How joyfully surprised I am to find Your majesty so tranquil and collected.

KING.

Surprised!

DOMINGO.

And heaven be thanked my fears were groundless! Now may I hope the best.

KING.

Your fears! What feared you?

DOMINGO.

I dare not hide it from your majesty That I had learned a secret----

KING (gloomily).

And have I Expressed a wish to share your secret with you?

Who ventures to anticipate me thus? Too forward, by mine honor!

DOMINGO.

Gracious monarch!

The place, the occasion, seal of secrecy 'Neath which I learned it--free me from this charge. It was intrusted to me at the seat Of penitence--intrusted as a crime That deeply weighed upon the tender soul Of the fair sinner who confessed her guilt, And sought the pardon of offended heaven. Too late the princess weeps a foul misdeed That may involve the queen herself in ruin.

KING.

Indeed! Kind soul! You have correctly guessed The occasion of your summons. You must guide me Through this dark labyrinth wherein blind zeal Has tangled me. From you I hope for truth. Be candid with me; what must I believe, And what determine? From your sacred office I look for strictest truth.

DOMINGO.

And if, my liege, The mildness ever incident to this My holy calling, did not such restraint Impose upon me, still I would entreat Your majesty, for your own peace of mind, To urge no further this discovery, And cease forever to pursue a secret Which never can be happily explained.

All that is yet discovered may be pardoned. Let the king say the word--and then the queen Has never sinned. The monarch's will bestows Virtue and fortune, both with equal ease.

And the king's undisturbed tranquillity Is, in itself, sufficient to destroy The rumors set on foot by calumny.

KING.

What! Rumors! and of me! among my subjects!

DOMINGO.

All falsehood, sire! Naught but the vilest falsehood! I'll swear 'tis false! Yet what's believed by all, Groundless and unconfirmed although it be, Works its effect, as sure as truth itself.

KING.

Not in this case, by heaven!

DOMINGO.

A virtuous name Is, after all, my liege, the only prize Which queens and peasants' wives contest together.

KING.

For which I surely have no need to tremble.

[He looks doubtingly at DOMINGO. After a pause. Priest, thou hast something fearful to impart.

Delay it not. I read it plainly stamped In thy ill-boding looks. Then out with it, Whate'er it be. Let me no longer tremble Upon the rack. What do the people say?

DOMINGO.

The people, sire, are liable to err, Nay err assuredly. What people think Should not alarm the king. Yet that they should Presume so far as to indulge such thoughts----

KING.

Why must I beg this poisonous draught so long?

DOMINGO.

The people often muse upon that month Which brought your majesty so near the grave, From that time, thirty weeks had scarce elapsed, Before the queen's delivery was announced.

[The KING rises and rings the bell. DUKE ALVA enters. DOMINGO alarmed.

I am amazed, your majesty! KING (going towards ALVA). Toledo!

You are a man--defend me from this priest!

DOMINGO (he and DUKE ALVA exchange embarrassed looks. After a pause). Could we have but foreseen that this occurrence

Would be avenged upon its mere relater.

KING.

Said you a bastard? I had scarce, you say, Escaped the pangs of death when first she felt She should, in nature's time, become a mother. Explain how this occurred! 'Twas then, if I Remember right, that you, in every church, Ordered devotions to St. Dominick, For the especial wonder he vouchsafed. On one side or the other, then, you lie! What would you have me credit? Oh, I see Full plainly through you now! If this dark plot Had then been ripe your saint had lost his fame.

ALVA.

This plot?

KING.

How can you with a harmony So unexampled in your very thoughts Concur, and not have first conspired together? Would you persuade me thus? Think you that I Perceived not with what eagerness you pounced Upon your prey? With what delight you fed Upon my pain,--my agony of grief?

Full well I marked the ardent, burning zeal With which the duke forestalled the mark of grace I destined for my son. And how this priest Presumed to fortify his petty spleen With my wrath's giant arm! I am, forsooth, A bow which each of you may bend at pleasure But I have yet a will. And if I needs Must doubt--perhaps I may begin with you.

ALVA.

Reward like this our truth did ne'er expect.

KING.

Your truth! Truth warns of apprehended danger. 'Tis malice that speaks only of the past.

What can I gain by your officiousness? Should your suspicion ripen to full truth, What follows but the pangs of separation, The melancholy triumphs of revenge?

But no: you only fear--you feed me with Conjectures vague. To hell's profound abyss You lead me on, then flee yourself away.

DOMINGO.

What other proofs than these are possible, When our own eyes can scarcely trust themselves? KING (after a long pause, turning earnestly and solemnly towards DOMINGO).

The grandees of the realm shall be convened, And I will sit in judgment. Then step forth In front of all, if you have courage for it, And charge her as a strumpet. She shall die--

Die without mercy--and the prince, too, with her! But mark me well: if she but clear herself That doom shall fall on you. Now, dare you show Honor to truth by such a sacrifice? Determine. No, you dare not. You are silent. Such is the zeal of liars!

ALVA

(who has stood at a distance, answers coldly and calmly). I will do it.

KING

(turns round with astonishment and looks at the DUKE for a long time without moving).

That's boldly said! But thou hast risked thy life In stubborn conflicts for far less a prize.

Has risked it with a gamester's recklessness-- For honor's empty bubble. What is lifemn To thee? I'll not expose the royal blood To such a madman's power, whose highest hope Must be to yield his wretched being up With some renown. I spurn your offer. Go; And wait my orders in the audience chamber.

[Exeunt.

SCENE V.

The KING alone.

Now give me, gracious Providence! a man.

Thou'st given me much already. Now vouchsafe me A man! for thou alone canst grant the boon.

Thine eye doth penetrate all hidden things Oh! give me but a friend: for I am not Omniscient like to thee. The ministers Whom thou hast chosen for me thou dost know-- And their deserts: and as their merits claim, I value them. Their subjugated vices, Coerced by rein severe, serve all my ends, As thy storms purify this nether world.

I thirst for truth. To reach its tranquil spring, Through the dark heaps of thick surrounding error, Is not the lot of kings. Give me the man, So rarely found, of pure and open heart, Of judgment clear, and eye unprejudiced, To aid me in the search. I cast the lots.

And may I find that man, among the thousands Who flutter in the sunshine of a court.

[He opens an escritoire and takes out a portfolio. After turning over the leaves a long time.

Nothing but names, mere names are here:--no note E'en of the services to which they owe

Their place upon the roll! Oh, what can be Of shorter memory than gratitude!

Here, in this other list, I read each fault Most accurately marked. That is not well! Can vengeance stand in need of such a help?

[He reads further.

Count Egmont! What doth he here? Long ago The victory of St. Quentin is forgotten.

I place him with the dead.

[He effaces this name and writes it on the other roll after he has read further.

The Marquis Posa!

The Marquis Posa! I can scarce recall This person to mind. And doubly marked!

A proof I destined him for some great purpose. How is it possible? This man, till now, Has ever shunned my presence--still has fled His royal debtor's eye? The only man, By heaven, within the compass of my realm, Who does not court my favor. Did he burn With avarice, or ambition, long ago He had appeared before my throne. I'll try This wondrous man. He who can thus dispense With royalty will doubtless speak the truth.

SCENE VI.

The Audience Chamber.

DON CARLOS in conversation with the PRINCE of PARMA. DUKES ALVA, FERIA, and MEDINA SIDONIA, COUNT LERMA, and other GRANDEES, with papers in their hands, awaiting the KING.

MEDINA SIDONIA (seems to be shunned by all the GRANDEES, turns towards DUKE ALVA, who, alone and absorbed in himself, walks up and down). Duke, you have had an audience of the king? How did you find him minded?

ALVA.

Somewhat ill For you, and for the news you bring.

MEDINA SIDONIA.

My heart Was lighter 'mid the roar of English cannon Than here on Spanish ground.

[CARLOS, who had regarded him with silent sympathy, now approaches him and presses his hand.

My warmest thanks, Prince, for this generous tear. You may perceive How all avoid me. Now my fate is sealed.

CARLOS.

Still hope the best both from my father's favor, And your own innocence.

MEDINA SIDONIA.

Prince, I have lost A fleet more mighty than e'er ploughed the waves. And what is such a head as mine to set 'Gainst seventy sunken galleons? And therewith Five hopeful sons! Alas! that breaks my heart.

SCENE VII.

The KING enters from his chamber, attired. The former all uncover and make room on both sides, while they form a semicircle round him. Silence.

KING (rapidly surveying the whole circle). Be covered, all.

[DON CARLOS and the PRINCE of PARMA approach first and kiss the KING's hand: he turns with friendly mien to the latter, taking no notice of his son.

Your mother, nephew, fain Would be informed what favor you have won Here in Madrid.

PARMA.

That question let her ask When I have fought my maiden battle, sire.

KING.

Be satisfied; your turn will come at last, When these old props decay.

[To the DUKE OF FERIA.

What brings you here?

FERIA (kneeling to the KING).

The master, sire, of Calatrava's order This morning died. I here return his cross.

KING (takes the order and looks round the whole circle). And who is worthiest after him to wear it?

[He beckons to DUKE ALVA, who approaches and bends on one knee. The KING hangs the order on his neck.

You are my ablest general! Ne'er aspire To more, and, duke, my favors shall not fail you. [He perceives the DUKE of MEDINA SIDONIA. My admiral!

MEDINA SIDONIA.

And here you see, great king, All that remains of the Armada's might, And of the flower of Spain. KING (after a pause). God rules above us! I sent you to contend with men, and not With rocks and storms. You're welcome to Madrid. [Extending his hand to him to kiss. I thank you for preserving in yourself A faithful servant to me. For as such I value him, my lords; and 'tis my will That you should honor him.

[He motions him to rise and cover himself, then turns to the others.

What more remains?

[To DON CARLOS and the PRINCE OF PARMA.

Princes, I thank you.

[They retire; the other GRANDEES approach, and kneeling, hand their papers to the KING. He looks over them rapidly, and hands them to DUKE ALVA.

Duke, let these be laid Before me in the council. Who waits further? [No one answers.

How comes it that amidst my train of nobles The Marquis Posa ne'er appears? I know This Marquis Posa served me with distinction. Does he still live? Why is he not among you?

LERMA.

The chevalier is just returned from travel, Completed through all Europe. He is now Here in Madrid, and waits a public day To cast himself before his sovereign's feet.

ALVA.

The Marquis Posa? Right, he is the same Bold Knight of Malta, sire, of whom renown Proclaims this gallant deed. Upon a summons Of the Grand Master, all the valiant knights Assembled in their island, at that time Besieged by Soliman. This noble youth, Scarce numbering eighteen summers, straightway fled From Alcala, where he pursued his studies, And suddenly arrived at La Valette.

"This Cross," he said, "was bought for me; and now To prove I'm worthy of it." He was one Of forty knights who held St. Elmo's Castle, At midday, 'gainst Piali, Ulucciali, And Mustapha, and Hassem; the assault Being thrice repeated. When the castle fell, And all the valiant knights were killed around him, He plunged into the ocean, and alone Reached La Valette in safety. Two months after The foe deserts the island, and the knight Returned to end his interrupted studies.

FERIA.

It was the Marquis Posa, too, who crushed The dread conspiracy in Catalonia; And by his marked activity preserved That powerful province to the Spanish crown.

KING.

I am amazed! What sort of man is this Who can deserve so highly, yet awake No pang of envy in the breasts of three Who speak his praise? The character he owns Must be of noble stamp indeed, or else

A very blank. I'm curious to behold This wondrous man.

[To DUKE ALVA.

Conduct him to the council When mass is over.

[Exit DUKE. The KING calls FERIA. And do you preside

Here in my place.

[Exit.

FERIA.

The king is kind to-day.

MEDIA SIDONIA.

Call him a god! So he has proved to me!

FERIA.

You well deserve your fortune, admiral! You have my warmest wishes.

ONE OF THE GRANDEES.

Sir, and mine.

A SECOND.

And also mine.

A THIRD.

My heart exults with joy-- So excellent a general!

THE FIRST.

The king

Showed you no kindness, 'twas your strict desert.

LERMA (to MEDINA SIDONIA, taking leave). Oh, how two little words have made your fortune!

[Exeunt all.

SCENE VIII.

The KING's Cabinet.

MARQUIS POSA and DUKE ALVA.

MARQUIS (as he enters).

Does he want me? What me? Impossible!

You must mistake the name. What can he want With me?

ALVA.

To know you.

MARQUIS.

Curiosity!

No more; I regret the precious minutes That I must lose: time passes swiftly by.

ALVA.

I now commend you to your lucky stars.

The king is in your hands. Employ this moment To your own best advantage; for, remember, If it is lost, you are alone to blame.

SCENE IX.

The MARQUIS alone.

MARQUIS.

Duke, 'tis well spoken! Turn to good account The moment which presents itself but once! Truly this courtier reads a useful lesson

If not in his sense good, at least in mine. [Walks a few steps backwards and forwards.

How came I here? Is it caprice or chance That shows me now my image in this mirror? Why, out of millions, should it picture me-- The most unlikely--and present my form

To the king's memory? Was this but chance? Perhaps 'twas something more!--what else is chance But the rude stone which from the sculptor's hand Receives its life? Chance comes from Providence, And man must mould it to his own designs.

What the king wants with me but little matters; I know the business I shall have with him.

Were but one spark of truth with boldness flung Into the despot's soul, how fruitful 'twere In the kind hand of Providence; and so What first appeared capricious act of chalice, May be designed for some momentous end. Whate'er it be, I'll act on this belief.

[He takes a few turns in the room, and stands at last in tranquil contemplation before a painting. The KING appears in the neighboring room, where he gives some orders. He then enters and stands motionless at the door, and contemplates the MARQUIS for some time without being observed.

SCENE X.

The KING, and MARQUIS POSA.

The MARQUIS, as soon as he observes the KING, comes forward and sinks on one knee; then rises and remains standing before him without any sign of confusion.

KING (looks at him with surprise). We've met before then?

MARQUIS.

No.

KING.

You did my crown Some service? Why then do you shun my thanks? My memory is thronged with suitor's claims.

One only is omniscient. 'Twas your duty To seek your monarch's eye! Why did you not?

MARQUIS.

Two days have scarce elapsed since my return From foreign travel, sire.

KING.

I would not stand Indebted to a subject; ask some favor----

MARQUIS.

I enjoy the laws.

KING.

So does the murderer!

MARQUIS.

Then how much more the honest citizen! My lot contents me, sire.

KING (aside).

By heavens! a proud And dauntless mind! That was to be expected. Proud I would have my Spaniards. Better far The cup should overflow than not be full.

They say you've left my service?

MARQUIS.

To make way For some one worthier, I withdrew.

KING.

'Tis pity. When spirits such as yours make holiday, The state must suffer. But perchance you feared To miss the post best suited to your merits.

MARQUIS.

Oh, no! I doubt not the experienced judge, In human nature skilled--his proper study,-- Will have discovered at a glance wherein

I may be useful to him, wherein not. With deepest gratitude, I feel the favor Wherewith, by so exalted an opinion, Your majesty is loading me; and yet---- [He pauses.

KING.

You hesitate?

MARQUIS.

I am, I must confess, Sire, at this moment, unprepared to clothe My thoughts, as the world's citizen, in phrase Beseeming to your subject. When I left The court forever, sire, I deemed myself Released from the necessity to give My reasons for this step.

KING.

Are they so weak?

What do you fear to risk by their disclosure?

MARQUIS.

My life at farthest, sire,--were time allowed For me to weary you--but this denied-- Then truth itself must suffer. I must choose 'Twixt your displeasure and contempt. And if I must decide, I rather would appear Worthy of punishment than pity.

KING

(with a look of expectation). Well?

MARQUIS.

I cannot be the servant of a prince.

[The KING looks at him with astonishment. I will not cheat the buyer. Should you deem Me worthy of your service, you prescribe A course of duty for me; you command My arm in battle and my head in council.

Then, not my actions, but the applause they meet At court becomes their object. But for me Virtue possesses an intrinsic worth. I would, myself, create that happiness

110

A monarch, with my hand, would seek to plant, And duty's task would prove an inward joy, And be my willing choice. Say, like you this?

And in your own creation could you hear A new creator? For I ne'er could stoop To be the chisel where I fain would be-- The sculptor's self. I dearly love mankind, My gracious liege, but in a monarchy

I dare not love another than myself.

KING.

This ardor is most laudable. You wish To do good deeds to others; how you do them Is but of small account to patriots, Or to the wise. Choose then within these realms The office where you best may satisfy This noble impulse.

MARQUIS.

'Tis not to be found.

KING.

How!

MARQUIS.

What your majesty would spread abroad, Through these my hands--is it the good of men? Is it the happiness that my pure love Would to mankind impart? Before such bliss Monarchs would tremble. No! Court policy Has raised up new enjoyments for mankind. Which she is always rich enough to grant; And wakened, in the hearts of men, new wishes Which such enjoyments only can content.

In her own mint she coins the truth--such truth! As she herself can tolerate: all forms Unlike her own are broken. But is that Which can content the court enough for me? Must my affection for my brother pledge Itself to work my brother injury?

To call him happy when he dare not think? Sire, choose not me to spread the happiness Which you have stamped for us. I must decline To circulate such coin. I cannot be The servant of a prince. KING (suddenly).

You are, perhaps, A Protestant?

MARQUIS (after some reflection). Our creeds, my liege, are one.

[A pause.

I am misunderstood. I feared as much. You see the veil torn by my hand aside From all the mysteries of majesty.

Who can assure you I shall still regard As sacred that which ceases to alarm me? I may seem dangerous, because I think Above myself. I am not so, my liege; My wishes lie corroding here. The rage

[Laying his hand on his breast. For innovation, which but serves to increase The heavy weight of chains it cannot break, Shall never fire my blood! The world is yet Unripe for my ideal; and I live A citizen of ages yet to come. But does a fancied picture break your rest? A breach of yours destroys it.

KING.

Say, am I The first to whom your views are known?

MARQUIS.

You are.

KING

(Rises, walks a few paces and then stops opposite the MARQUIS--aside). This tone, at least, is new; but flattery Exhausts itself. And men of talent still Disdain to imitate. So let us test Its opposite for once. Why should I not? There is a charm in novelty. Should we Be so agreed, I will bethink me now Of some new state employment, in whose duties Your powerful mind----

MARQUIS.

Sire, I perceive how small, How mean, your notions are of manly worth. Suspecting, in an honest man's discourse, Naught but a flatterer's artifice—methinks I can explain the cause of this your error. Mankind compel you to it. With free choice They have disclaimed their true nobility, Lowered themselves to their degraded state. Before man's inward worth, as from a phantom, They fly in terror--and contented with Their poverty, they ornament their chains With slavish prudence; and they call it virtue To bear them with a show of resignation. Thus did you find the world, and thus it was By your great father handed o'er to you. In this debased connection--how could you Respect mankind?

KING.

Your words contain some truth.

MARQUIS.

Alas! that when from the Creator's hand You took mankind, and moulded him to suit Your own ideas, making yourself the god Of this new creature, you should overlook That you yourself remained a human being-- A very man, as from God's hands you came. Still did you feel a mortal's wants and pains.

You needed sympathy; but to a God One can but sacrifice, and pray, and tremble-- Wretched exchange! Perversion most unblest Of sacred nature! Once degrade mankind, And make him but a thing to play upon, Who then can share the harmony with you?

KING (aside).

By heaven, he moves me!

MARQUIS.

But this sacrifice

To you is valueless. You thus become A thing apart, a species of your own.

This is the price you pay for being a god; 'Twere dreadful were it not so, and if you Gained nothing by the misery of millions! And if the very freedom you destroyed Were the sole blessing that could make you happy. Dismiss me, sire, I pray you; for my theme Bears me too far; my heart is full; too strong The charm, to stand before the only man To whom I may reveal it.

[The COUNT LERMA enters, and whispers a few words to the KING, who signs him to withdraw, and continues sitting in his former posture.

KING (to the MARQUIS, after LERMA is gone). Nay, continue.

MARQUIS (after a pause). I feel, sire--all the worth----

KING.

Proceed; you had Yet more to say to me.

MARQUIS.

Your majesty, I lately passed through Flanders and Brabant, So many rich and blooming provinces, Filled with a valiant, great, and honest people. To be the father of a race like this I thought must be divine indeed; and then I stumbled on a heap of burnt men's bones.

[He stops, he fixes a penetrating look on the KING, who endeavors to return his glance; but he looks on the ground, embarrassed and confused.

True, you are forced to act so; but that you Could dare fulfil your task--this fills my soul With shuddering horror! Oh, 'tis pity that The victim, weltering in his blood, must cease To chant the praises of his sacrificer!

And that mere men--not beings loftier far-- Should write the history of the world. But soon A milder age will follow that of Philip, An age of truer wisdom; hand in hand,

The subjects' welfare and the sovereign's greatness Will walk in union. Then the careful state Will spare her children, and necessity No longer glory to be thus inhuman.

KING.

When, think you, would that blessed age arrive, If I had shrunk before the curse of this? Behold my Spain, see here the burgher's good Blooms in eternal and unclouded peace. A peace like this will I bestow on Flanders.

MARQUIS (hastily).

The churchyard's peace! And do you hope to end What you have now begun? Say, do you hope To check the ripening change of Christendom, The universal spring, that shall renew

The earth's fair form? Would you alone, in Europe, Fling yourself down before the rapid wheel Of destiny, which rolls its ceaseless course, And seize its spokes with human arm. Vain thought! Already thousands have your kingdom fled In joyful poverty: the honest burgher For his faith exiled, was your noblest subject! See! with a mother's arms, Elizabeth Welcomes the fugitives, and Britain blooms In rich luxuriance, from our country's arts.

Bereft of the new Christian's industry, Granada lies forsaken, and all Europe Exulting, sees his foe oppressed with wounds, By its own hands inflicted!

[The KING is moved; the MARQUIS observes it, and advances a step nearer.

You would plant For all eternity, and yet the seeds You sow around you are the seeds of death! This hopeless task, with nature's laws at strife, Will ne'er survive the spirit of its founder.

You labor for ingratitude; in vain, With nature you engage in desperate struggle-- In vain you waste your high and royal life In projects of destruction. Man is greatern Than you esteem him. He will burst the chains Of a long slumber, and reclaim once more His just and hallowed rights. With Nero's name, And fell Busiris', will he couple yours; And--ah! you once deserved a better fate.

KING.

How know you that?

MARQUIS.

In very truth you did-- Yes, I repeat it--by the Almighty power! Restore us all you have deprived us of, And, generous as strong, let happiness Flow from your horn of plenty--let man's mind Ripen in your vast empire--give us back All you have taken from us--and become, Amidst a thousand kings, a king indeed! [He advances boldly, and fixes on him a look of earnestness and enthusiasm. Oh, that the eloquence of all those myriads, Whose fate depends on this momentous hour, Could hover on my lips, and fan the spark That lights thine eye into a glorious flame! Renounce the mimicry of godlike powers Which level us to nothing. Be, in truth, An image of the Deity himself!

Never did mortal man possess so much For purpose so divine. The kings of Europe Pay homage to the name of Spain. Be you The leader of these kings. One pen-stroke now, One motion of your hand, can new create The earth! but grant us liberty of thought.

[Casts himself at his feet. KING (surprised, turns away his face, then again looks towards the MARQUIS). Enthusiast most strange! arise; but I----

MARQUIS.

Look round on all the glorious face of nature, On freedom it is founded--see how rich, Through freedom it has grown. The great Creator Bestows upon the worm its drop of dew, And gives free-will a triumph in abodes Where lone corruption reigns. See your creation, How small, how poor! The rustling of a leaf Alarms the mighty lord of Christendom.

Each virtue makes you quake with fear. While he, Not to disturb fair freedom's blest appearance, Permits the frightful ravages of evil To waste his fair domains. The great Creator We see not--he conceals himself within His own eternal laws. The sceptic sees Their operation, but beholds not Him. "Wherefore a God!" he cries, "the world itself Suffices for itself!" And Christian prayer Ne'er praised him more than doth this blasphemy.

KING.

And will you undertake to raise up this Exalted standard of weak human nature In my dominions?

MARQUIS.

You can do it, sire.

Who else? Devote to your own people's bliss The kingly power, which has too long enriched The greatness of the throne alone. Restore The prostrate dignity of human nature, And let the subject be, what once he was, The end and object of the monarch's care, Bound by no duty, save a brother's love. And when mankind is to itself restored, Roused to a sense of its own innate worth,

When freedom's lofty virtues proudly flourish-- Then, sire, when you have made your own wide realms The happiest in the world, it then may be Your duty to subdue the universe.

KING (after a long pause).

I've heard you to the end. Far differently I find, than in the minds of other men, The world exists in yours. And you shall not By foreign laws be judged. I am the first To whom you have your secret self disclosed; I know it--so believe it--for the sake Of this forbearance--that you have till now Concealed these sentiments, although embraced With so much ardor,--for this cautious prudence.

I will forget, young man, that I have learned them, And how I learned them. Rise! I will confute Your youthful dreams by my matured experience, Not by my power as king. Such is my will, And therefore act I thus. Poison itself May, in a worthy nature, be transformed To some benignant use. But, sir, beware My Inquisition! 'Twould afflict me much----

MARQUIS.

Indeed!

KING (lost in surprise).

Ne'er met I such a man as that! No, marquis, no! you wrong me! Not to you Will I become a Nero--not to you!-- All happiness shall not be blasted round me, And you at least, beneath my very eyes, May dare continue to remain a man.

MARQUIS (quickly).

And, sire, my fellow-subjects? Not for me, Nor my own cause, I pleaded. Sire! your subjects----

KING.

Nay, if you know so well how future times Will judge me, let them learn at least from you, That when I found a man, I could respect him.

MARQUIS.

Oh, let not the most just of kings at once

Be the most unjust! In your realm of Flanders There are a thousand better men than I.

But you--sire! may I dare to say so much-- For the first time, perhaps, see liberty In milder form portrayed. KING (with gentle severity).

No more of this, Young man! You would, I know, think otherwise Had you but learned to understand mankind As I. But truly--I would not this meeting Should prove our last. How can I hope to win you?

MARQUIS.

Pray leave me as I am. What value, sire, Should I be to you were you to corrupt me?

KING.

This pride I will not bear. From this day forth I hold you in my service. No remonstrance-- For I will have it so.

[After a pause. But how is this?

What would I now? Was it not truth I wished?

But here is something more. Marquis, so far You've learned to know me as a king; but yet You know me not as man-- [The MARQUIS seems to meditate. I understand you-- Were I the most unfortunate of fathers, Yet as a husband may I not be blest?

MARQUIS.

If the possession of a hopeful son, And a most lovely spouse, confer a claim On mortal to assume that title, sire, In both respects, you are supremely blest. KING (with a serious look).

That am I not--and never, till this hour, Have I so deeply felt that I am not so.

[Contemplating the MARQUIS with a look of melancholy.

MARQUIS.

The prince possesses a right noble mind. I ne'er have known him otherwise.

KING.

I have

The treasure he has robbed me of, no crown Can e'er requite. So virtuous a queen!

MARQUIS.

Who dare assert it, sire?

KING.

The world! and scandal! And I myself! Here lie the damning proofs Of doubtless guilt-- and others, too, exist, From which I fear the worst. But still 'tis hard To trust one proof alone. Who brings the charge? And oh! if this were possible--that she, The queen, so foully could pollute her honor, Then how much easier were it to believe An Eboli may be a slanderer!

Does not that priest detest my son and her? And can I doubt that Alva broods revenge? My wife has higher worth than all together.

MARQUIS.

And there exists besides in woman's soul A treasure, sire, beyond all outward show, Above the reach of slander--female virtue!

KING.

Marquis! those thoughts are mine. It costs too much To sink so low as they accuse the queen.

The sacred ties of honor are not broken With so much ease, as some would fain persuade me. Marquis, you know mankind. Just such a man As you I long have wished for--you are kind-- Cheerful--and deeply versed in human nature-- Therefore I've chosen you----

MARQUIS (surprised and alarmed). Me, sire!

KING.

You stand Before your king and ask no special favor-- For yourself nothing!--that is new to me-- You will be just--ne'er weakly swayed by passion. Watch my son close--search the queen's inmost heart. You shall have power to speak with her in private.

Retire.

[He rings a bell.

MARQUIS.

And if with but one hope fulfilled I now depart, then is this day indeed The happiest of my life.

KING

(Holds out his hand to him to kiss). I hold it not Amongst my days a lost one.

[The MARQUIS rises and goes. COUNT LERMA enters. Count, in future, The marquis is to enter, unannounced.

ACT IV.

SCENE I.

The Queen's Apartment.

QUEEN, DUCHESS OLIVAREZ, PRINCESS EBOLI, COUNTESS FUENTES.

QUEEN (to the first lady as she rises).

And so the key has not been found! My casket Must be forced open then--and that at once.

[She observes PRINCESS EBOLI, who approaches and kisses her hand. Welcome, dear princess! I rejoice to see you So near recovered. But you still look pale.

FUENTES (with malice).

The fault of that vile fever which affects The nerves so painfully. Is't not, princess?

QUEEN.

I wished to visit you, dear Eboli, But dared not.

OLIVAREZ.

Oh! the Princess Eboli Was not in want of company.

QUEEN.

Why, that I readily believe, but what's the matter? You tremble----

PRINCESS.

Nothing--nothing, gracious queen. Permit me to retire.

QUEEN.

You hide it from us-- And are far worse than you would have us think. Standing must weary you. Assist her, countess, And let her rest awhile upon that seat.

PRINCESS (going).

I shall be better in the open air.

QUEEN.

Attend her, countess. What a sudden illness!

[A PAGE enters and speaks to the DUCHESS, who then addresses the QUEEN.

OLIVAREZ.

The Marquis Posa waits, your majesty, With orders from the king.

QUEEN.

Admit him then.

[PAGE admits the MARQUIS and exit.

SCENE II.

MARQUIS POSA. The former.

The MARQUIS falls on one knee before the QUEEN, who signs to him to rise.

QUEEN.

What are my lord's commands? And may I dare Thus publicly to hear----

My business is In private with your royal majesty.

[The ladies retire on a signal from the QUEEN.

SCENE III.

The QUEEN, MARQUIS POSA.

QUEEN (full of astonishment).

How! Marquis, dare I trust my eyes? Are you Commissioned to me from the king?

MARQUIS.

Does this

Seem such a wonder to your majesty? To me 'tis otherwise.

QUEEN.

The world must sure Have wandered from its course! That you and he-- I must confess-

MARQUIS.

It does sound somewhat strange-- But be it so. The present times abound In prodigies.

QUEEN.

But none can equal this.

Suppose I had at last allowed myself To be converted, and had weary grown Of playing the eccentric at the court Of Philip. The eccentric! What is that?

He who would be of service to mankind Must first endeavor to resemble them.

What end is gained by the vain-glorious garb Of the sectarian? Then suppose--for who From vanity is so completely free As for his creed to seek no proselytes? Suppose, I say, I had it in my mind To place my own opinions on the throne!

QUEEN.

No, marquis! no! Not even in jest could I Suspect you of so wild a scheme as this; No visionary you! to undertake What you can ne'er accomplish.

MARQUIS.

But that seems To be the very point at issue.

QUEEN.

What I chiefly blame you, marquis, for, and what Could well estrange me from you--is---

MARQUIS.

Perhaps Duplicity!

QUEEN.

At least--a want of candor.

Perhaps the king himself has no desire You should impart what now you mean to tell me.

MARQUIS.

No.

QUEEN.

And can evil means be justified By honest ends? And--pardon me the doubt-- Can your high bearing stoop to such an office? I scarce can think it.

MARQUIS.

Nor, indeed, could I, Were my sole purpose to deceive the king. 'Tis not my wish--I mean to serve him now More honestly than he himself commands.

QUEEN.

'Tis spoken like yourself. Enough of this-- What would the king?

MARQUIS.

The king? I can, it seems, Retaliate quickly on my rigid judge And what I have deferred so long to tell, Your majesty, perhaps, would willingly Longer defer to hear. But still it must Be heard. The king requests your majesty Will grant no audience to the ambassador Of France to-day. Such were my high commands-- They're executed.

QUEEN.

Marquis, is that all You have to tell me from him?

MARQUIS.

Nearly all That justifies me thus to seek your presence.

QUEEN.

Well, marquis, I'm contented not to hear What should, perhaps, remain a secret from me.

MARQUIS.

True, queen! though were you other than yourself, I should inform you straight of certain things-- Warn you of certain men--but this to you Were a vain office. Danger may arise And disappear around you, unperceived. You will not know it--of too little weight To chase the slumber from your angel brow.

But 'twas not this, in sooth, that brought me hither, Prince Carlos----

QUEEN.

What of him? How have you left him?

MARQUIS.

E'en as the only wise man of his time, In whom it is a crime to worship truth-- And ready, for his love to risk his life, As the wise sage for his. I bring few words-- But here he is himself.

[Giving the QUEEN a letter. QUEEN (after she has read it). He says he must

Speak with me----

MARQUIS.

So do I.

QUEEN.

And will he thus Be happy--when he sees with his own eyes, That I am wretched?

MARQUIS.

No; but more resolved, More active.

QUEEN.

How?

MARQUIS.

Duke Alva is appointed To Flanders.

QUEEN.

Yes, appointed--so I hear.

MARQUIS.

The king cannot retract:--we know the king. This much is clear, the prince must not remain Here in Madrid, nor Flanders be abandoned.

QUEEN.

And can you hinder it?

MARQUIS.

Perhaps I can,

But then the means are dangerous as the evil-- Rash as despair--and yet I know no other.

QUEEN.

Name them.

MARQUIS.

To you, and you alone, my queen, Will I reveal them; for from you alone, Carlos will hear them named without a shudder. The name they bear is somewhat harsh.

QUEEN.

Rebellion!

MARQUIS.

He must prove faithless to the king, and fly With secrecy to Brussels, where the Flemings Wait him with open arms. The Netherlands Will rise at his command. Our glorious cause From the king's son will gather matchless strength, The Spanish throne shall tremble at his arms, And what his sire denied him in Madrid, That will he willingly concede in Brussels.

QUEEN.

You've spoken with the king to-day--and yet Maintain all this.

MARQUIS.

Yes, I maintain it all, Because I spoke with him.

QUEEN

(After a pause). The daring plan Alarms and pleases me. You may be right--

The thought is bold, and that perhaps enchants me. Let it but ripen. Does Prince Carlos know it?

MARQUIS.

It was my wish that he should hear it first From your own lips.

QUEEN.

The plan is doubtless good, But then the prince's youth----

MARQUIS.

No disadvantage!

He there will find the bravest generals Of the Emperor Charles--an Egmont and an Orange-- In battle daring, and in council wise.

QUEEN (with vivacity).

True--the design is grand and beautiful! The prince must act; I feel it sensibly.

The part he's doomed to play here in Madrid Has bowed me to the dust on his account.

I promise him the aid of France and Savoy; I think with you, lord marquis--he must act-- But this design needs money----

MARQUIS.

It is ready.

QUEEN.

I, too, know means.

MARQUIS.

May I then give him hopes Of seeing you?

QUEEN.

I will consider it.

MARQUIS.

The prince, my queen, is urgent for an answer. I promised to procure it.

[Presenting his writing tablet to the QUEEN. Two short lines Will be enough.

QUEEN (after she has written).

When do we meet again?

MARQUIS.

Whene'er you wish.

QUEEN.

Whene'er I wish it, marquis!

How can I understand this privilege?

MARQUIS.

As innocently, queen, as e'er you may. But we enjoy it--that is sure enough.

QUEEN (interrupting).

How will my heart rejoice should this become A refuge for the liberties of Europe, And this through him! Count on my silent aid!

MARQUIS (with animation).

Right well I knew your heart would understand me. [The DUCHESS OLIVAREZ enters.

QUEEN (coldly to the MARQUIS).

My lord! the king's commands I shall respect As law. Assure him of the queen's submission.

[She makes a sign to him. Exit MARQUIS.

SCENE IV.

A Gallery.

DON CARLOS, COUNT LERMA.

CARLOS.

Here we are undisturbed. What would you now Impart to me?

LERMA.

Your highness has a friend Here at the court.

CARLOS (starting).

A friend! I knew it not! But what's your meaning?

LERMA.

I must sue for pardon That I am learned in more than I should know. But for your highness' comfort I've received it From one I may depend upon--in short,

I have it from myself.

CARLOS.

Whom speak you of?

LERMA.

The Marquis Posa.

CARLOS.

What!

LERMA.

And if your highness Has trusted to him more of what concerns you Than every one should know, as I am led To fear----

CARLOS.

You fear!

LERMA.

He has been with the king.

CARLOS.

Indeed!

LERMA.

Two hours in secret converse too.

CARLOS.

Indeed!

LERMA.

The subject was no trifling matter.

CARLOS.

That I can well believe.

LERMA.

And several times I heard your name.

CARLOS.

That's no bad sign, I hope.

LERMA.

And then, this morning, in the king's apartment, The queen was spoken of mysteriously.

CARLOS (starts back astonished). Count Lerma!

LERMA.

When the marquis had retired I was commanded to admit his lordship In future unannounced.

CARLOS.

Astonishing!

LERMA.

And without precedent do I believe, Long as I served the king----

CARLOS.

'Tis strange, indeed!

How did you say the queen was spoken of?

LERMA (steps back).

No, no, my prince! that were against my duty.

CARLOS.

'Tis somewhat strange! One secret you impart. The other you withhold.

LERMA.

The first was due To you, the other to the king.

CARLOS.

You're right.

LERMA.

And still I've thought you, prince, a man of honor.

CARLOS.

Then you have judged me truly.

LERMA.

But all virtue

Is spotless till it's tried.

CARLOS.

Some stand the trial.

LERMA.

A powerful monarch's favor is a prize Worth seeking for; and this alluring bait Has ruined many a virtue.

CARLOS.

Truly said!

LERMA.

And oftentimes 'tis prudent to discover-- What scarce can longer be concealed.

CARLOS.

Yes, prudent It may be, but you say you've ever known The marquis prove himself a man of honor.

LERMA.

And if he be so still my fears are harmless, And you become a double gainer, prince.

[Going.

CARLOS (follows him with emotion, and presses his hand). Trebly I gain, upright and worthy man, I gain another friend, nor lose the one Whom I before possessed.

[Exit LERMA.

SCENE V.

MARQUIS POSA comes through the gallery. CARLOS.

MARQUIS.

Carlos! My Carlos!

CARLOS.

Who calls me? Ah! 'tis thou--I was in haste To gain the convent! You will not delay.

[Going.

MARQUIS.

Hold! for a moment.

CARLOS.

We may be observed.

MARQUIS.

No chance of that. 'Tis over now. The queen----

CARLOS.

You've seen my father.

MARQUIS.

Yes! he sent for me.

CARLOS (full of expectation). Well!

MARQUIS.

'Tis all settled--you may see the queen.

CARLOS.

Yes! but the king! What said the king to you?

MARQUIS.

Not much. Mere curiosity to learn My history. The zeal of unknown friends-- I know not what. He offered me employment.

CARLOS.

Which you, of course, rejected?

MARQUIS.

Yes, of course

CARLOS.

How did you separate?

MARQUIS.

Oh, well enough!

CARLOS.

And was I mentioned?

MARQUIS.

Yes; in general terms.

[Taking out a pocketbook and giving it to the PRINCE. See here are two lines written by the queen,

To-morrow I will settle where and how.

CARLOS (reads it carelessly, puts the tablet in his pocket, and is going).

You'll meet me at the prior's?

MARQUIS.

Yes! But stay Why in such haste? No one is coming hither.

CARLOS (with a forced smile).

Have we in truth changed characters? To-day You seem so bold and confident.

MARQUIS.

To-day-- Wherefore to-day?

CARLOS.

What writes the queen to me?

MARQUIS.

Have you not read this instant?

CARLOS.

I? Oh yes.

MARQUIS.

What is't disturbs you now?

CARLOS (reads the tablet again, delighted and fervently). Angel of Heaven!

I will be so,--I will be worthy of thee.

Love elevates great minds. So come what may, Whatever thou commandest, I'll perform.

She writes that I must hold myself prepared For a great enterprise! What can she mean? Dost thou not know?

MARQUIS.

And, Carlos, if I knew, Say, art thou now prepared to hear it from me?

CARLOS.

Have I offended thee? I was distracted. Roderigo, pardon me.

MARQUIS.

Distracted! How?

CARLOS.

I scarcely know! But may I keep this tablet?

MARQUIS.

Not so! I came to ask thee for thine own.

CARLOS.

My tablet! Why?

MARQUIS.

And whatsoever writings You have, unfit to meet a stranger's eye-- Letters or memorandums, and in short, Your whole portfolio.

CARLOS.

Why?

MARQUIS.

That we may be Prepared for accidents. Who can prevent Surprise? They'll never seek them in my keeping. Here, give them to me----

CARLOS

(Uneasy). Strange! What can it mean?

MARQUIS.

Be not alarmed! 'Tis nothing of importance A mere precaution to prevent surprise. You need not be alarmed!

CARLOS

(Gives him the portfolio). Be careful of it.

MARQUIS.

Be sure I will.

CARLOS (looks at him significantly). I give thee much, Roderigo!

MARQUIS.

Not more than I have often had from thee. The rest we'll talk of yonder. Now farewell.

[Going.

CARLOS

(Struggling with himself, then calls him back). Give me my letters back; there's one amongst them The queen addressed to me at Alcala, When I was sick to death. Still next my heart I carry it; to take this letter from me Goes to my very soul. But leave me that, And take the rest.

[He takes it out, and returns the portfolio.

MARQUIS.

I yield unwillingly-- For 'twas that letter which I most required.

CARLOS.

Farewell!

[He goes away slowly, stops a moment at the door, turns back again, and brings him the letter.

You have it there.

[His hand trembles, tears start from his eyes, he falls on the neck of the MARQUIS, and presses his face to his bosom.

Oh, not my father, Could do so much, Roderigo! Not my father! [Exit hastily.

SCENE VI.

MARQUIS (looks after him with astonishment). And is this possible! And to this hour Have I not known him fully? In his heart This blemish has escaped my eye. Distrust Of me--his friend! But no, 'tis calumny!

What hath he done that I accuse him thus Of weakest weakness. I myself commit The fault I charge on him. What have I done Might well surprise him! When hath he displayed To his best friend such absolute reserve?

Carlos, I must afflict thee--there's no help-- And longer still distress thy noble soul.

In me the king hath placed his confidence, His holiest trust reposed--as in a casket, And this reliance calls for gratitude. How can disclosure serve thee when my silence Brings thee no harm--serves thee, perhaps? Ah! why Point to the traveller the impending storm?

Enough, if I direct its anger past thee!

And when thou wakest the sky's again serene.

[Exit.

SCENE VII.

The KING's Cabinet.

The KING seated, near him the INFANTA CLARA EUGENIA.

KING (after a deep silence).

No--she is sure my daughter--or can nature Thus lie like truth! Yes, that blue eye is mine! And I am pictured in thy every feature.

Child of my love! for such thou art--I fold thee Thus to my heart; thou art my blood.

[Starts and pauses: My blood--

What's worse to fear? Are not my features his?

[Takes the miniature in his hand and looks first at the portrait, then at the mirror opposite; at last he throws it on the ground, rises hastily, and pushes the INFANTA from him.

Away, away! I'm lost in this abyss.

SCENE VIII.

COUNT LERMA and the KING.

LERMA.

Her majesty is in the antechamber.

KING.

What! Now?

LERMA.

And begs the favor of an audience.

KING.

Now! At this unaccustomed hour! Not now-- I cannot see her yet.

LERMA.

Here comes the queen. [Exit LERMA.

SCENE IX.

The KING, the QUEEN enters, and the INFANTA.

The INFANTA runs to meet the QUEEN and clings to her; the QUEEN falls at the KING's feet, who is silent, and appears confused and embarrassed.

QUEEN.

My lord! My husband! I'm constrained to seek Justice before the throne!

KING.

What? Justice!

QUEEN.

Yes!

I'm treated with dishonor at the court! My casket has been rifled.

KING.

What! Your casket?

QUEEN.

And things I highly value have been plundered.

KING.

Things that you highly value.

QUEEN.

From the meaning

Which ignorant men's officiousness, perhaps, Might give to them----

KING.

What's this? Officiousness, And meaning! How? But rise.

QUEEN.

Oh no, my husband!

Not till you bind yourself by sacred promise, By virtue of your own authority, To find the offender out, and grant redress, Or else dismiss my suite, which hides a thief.

KING.

But rise! In such a posture! Pray you, rise.

QUEEN (rises).

'Tis some one of distinction--I know well; My casket held both diamonds and pearls Of matchless value, but he only took My letters.

KING.

May I ask----

QUEEN.

Undoubtedly, My husband. They were letters from the prince: His miniature as well.

KING.

From whom?

QUEEN.

The prince, Your son.

KING.

To you?

QUEEN.

Sent by the prince to me.

KING.

What! From Prince Carlos! Do you tell me that?

QUEEN.

Why not tell you, my husband?

KING.

And not blush.

QUEEN.

What mean you? You must surely recollect The letters Carlos sent me to St. Germains, With both courts' full consent. Whether that leave Extended to the portrait, or alone

His hasty hope dictated such a step, I cannot now pretend to answer; but If even rash, it may at least be pardoned For thus much I may be his pledge--that then He never thought the gift was for his mother.

[Observes the agitation of the KING. What moves you? What's the matter?

INFANTA (who has found the miniature on the ground, and has been playing with it, brings it to the QUEEN).

Look, dear mother!

See what a pretty picture!

QUEEN.

What then my---- [She recognizes the miniature, and remains in speechless astonishment. They both gaze at each other. After a long pause.

In truth, this mode of trying a wife's heart Is great and royal, sire! But I should wish To ask one question?

KING.

'Tis for me to question.

QUEEN.

Let my suspicions spare the innocent.

And if by your command this theft was done----

KING.

It was so done!

QUEEN.

Then I have none to blame, And none to pity--other than yourself-- Since you possess a wife on whom such schemes Are thrown away.

KING.

This language is not new-- Nor shall you, madam, now again deceive me As in the gardens of Aranjuez-- My queen of angel purity, who then So haughtily my accusation spurned-- I know her better now.

QUEEN.

What mean you, sire?

KING.

Madam! thus briefly and without reserve-- Say is it true? still true, that you conversed With no one there? Is really that the truth?

QUEEN.

I spoke there with the prince.

KING.

Then is clear As day! So daring! heedless of mine honor!

QUEEN.

Your honor, sire! If that be now the question, A greater honor is, methinks, at stake Than Castile ever brought me as a dowry.

KING.

Why did you then deny the prince's presence?

QUEEN.

Because I'm not accustomed to be questioned Like a delinquent before all your courtiers; I never shall deny the truth when asked With kindness and respect. Was that the tone Your majesty used towards me in Aranjuez? Are your assembled grandees the tribunal Queens must account to for their private conduct? I gave the prince the interview he sought With earnest prayer, because, my liege and lord, I--the queen--wished and willed it, and because I never can admit that formal custom Should sit as judge on actions that are guiltless; And I concealed it from your majesty Because I chose not to contend with you About this right in presence of your courtiers.

KING.

You speak with boldness, madam!

QUEEN.

I may add, Because the prince, in his own father's heart, Scarce finds that kindness he so well deserves.

KING.

So well deserves!

QUEEN.

Why, sire! should I conceal it!

Highly do I esteem him--yes! and love him As a most dear relation, who was once Deemed worthy of a dearer--tenderer--title. I've yet to learn that he, on this account, Should be estranged from me beyond all others,-- Because he once was better loved than they.

Though your state policy may knit together What bands it pleases--'tis a harder task To burst such ties! I will not hate another For any one's command--and since I must So speak--such dictates I will not endure.

KING.

Elizabeth! you've seen me in weak moments-- And their remembrance now emboldens you. On that strong influence you now depend, Which you have often, with so much success, Against my firmness tried. But fear the more The power which has seduced me to be weak May yet inflame me to some act of madness.

QUEEN.

What have I done? KING (takes her hand).

If it should prove but so-- And is it not already? If the full Accumulated measure of your guilt Become but one breath heavier--should I be Deceived----

[Lets her hand go. I can subdue these last remains Of weakness--can and will--then woe betide Myself and you, Elizabeth!

QUEEN.

What crime Have I committed?

KING.

On my own account then Shall blood be shed.

QUEEN.

And has it come to this? Oh, Heaven!

KING.

I shall forget myself--I shall

Regard no usage and no voice of nature-- Not e'en the law of nations.

QUEEN.

Oh, how much I pity you!

KING.

The pity of a harlot!

INFANTA (clinging to her mother in terror). The king is angry, and my mother weeps.

[KING pushes the child violently from the QUEEN.

QUEEN (with mildness and dignity, but with faltering voice). This child I must protect from cruelty--

Come with me, daughter. [Takes her in her arms.

If the king no more Acknowledge thee--beyond the Pyrenees I'll call protectors to defend our cause.

[Going.

KING (embarrassed). Queen!

QUEEN.

I can bear no more--it is too much!

[Hastening to the door, she falls with her child on the threshold. KING (running to her assistance).

Heavens! What is that? INFANTA (cries out with terror). She bleeds! My mother bleeds!

[Runs out.

KING (anxiously assisting her).

Oh, what a fearful accident! You bleed; Do I deserve this cruel punishment?

Rise and collect yourself--rise, they are coming! They will surprise us! Shall the assembled court Divert themselves with such a spectacle?

Must I entreat you? Rise.

[She rises, supported by the KING.

SCENE X.

The former, ALVA, DOMINGO entering, alarmed, ladies follow.

KING.

Now let the queen Be led to her apartment; she's unwell.

[Exit the QUEEN, attended by her ladies. ALVA and DOMINGO come forward.

ALVA.

The queen in tears, and blood upon her face!

KING.

Does that surprise the devils who've misled me?

ALVA and DOMINGO.

We?

KING.

You have said enough to drive me mad. But nothing to convince me.

ALVA.

We gave you What we ourselves possessed.

KING.

May hell reward you!

I've done what I repent of! Ah! was hers, The language of a conscience dark with guilt?

MARQUIS POSA (from without). Say, can I see the king?

SCENE XI.

The former, MARQUIS POSA.

KING (starts up at the sound of his voice, and advances some paces to meet him).

Ah! here he comes.

Right welcome, marquis! Duke! I need you now No longer. Leave us.

[ALVA and DOMINGO look at each other with silent astonishment and retire.

SCENE XII.

The KING, and MARQUIS POSA.

MARQUIS.

That old soldier, sire, Who has faced death, in twenty battles, for you, Must hold it thankless to be so dismissed.

KING.

'Tis thus for you to think--for me to act; In a few hours you have been more to me Than that man in a lifetime. Nor shall I Keep my content a secret. On your brow The lustre of my high and royal favor Shall shine resplendent--I will make that man A mark for envy whom I choose my friend.

MARQUIS.

What if the veil of dark obscurity Were his sole claim to merit such a title?

KING.

What come you now to tell me?

MARQUIS.

As I passed Along the antechamber a dread rumor Fell on my ear,--it seemed incredible,-- Of a most angry quarrel--blood--the queen----

KING.

Come you from her?

MARQUIS.

I should be horrified Were not the rumor false: or should perhaps Your majesty meantime have done some act-- Discoveries of importance I have made, Which wholly change the aspect of affairs.

KING.

How now?

MARQUIS.

I found an opportunity

To seize your son's portfolio, with his letters, Which, as I hope, may throw some light----

[He gives the PRINCE's portfolio to the KING. KING (looks through it eagerly).

A letter

From the emperor, my father. How I a letter Of which I ne'er remember to have heard.

[He reads it through, puts it aside, and goes to the other papers.

A drawing of some fortress--detached thoughts From Tacitus--and what is here? The hand I surely recognize--it is a lady's.

[He reads it attentively, partly to himself, and partly aloud.

"This key--the farthest chamber of the queen's Pavilion!" Ha! what's this? "The voice of love,-- The timid lover--may--a rich reward."

Satanic treachery! I see it now. 'Tis she--'tis her own writing!

MARQUIS.

The queen's writing! Impossible!

KING.

The Princess Eboli's.

MARQUIS.

Then, it was true, what the queen's page confessed, Not long since--that he brought this key and letter.

KING (grasping the MARQUIS' hand in great emotion). Marquis! I see that I'm in dreadful hands.

This woman--I confess it--'twas this woman Forced the queen's casket: and my first suspicions Were breathed by her. Who knows how deep the priest May be engaged in this? I am deceived By cursed villany.

MARQUIS.

Then it was lucky----

KING.

Marquis! O marquis! I begin to fear I've wronged my wife.

MARQUIS.

If there exist between The prince and queen some secret understandings, They are of other import, rest assured, Than those they charge her with. I know, for certain, The prince's prayer to be despatched to Flanders Was by the queen suggested.

KING.

I have thought so.

MARQUIS.

The queen's ambitious. Dare I speak more fully? She sees, with some resentment, her high hopes All disappointed, and herself shut out From share of empire. Your son's youthful ardor Offers itself to her far-reaching views, Her heart! I doubt if she can love.

KING.

Her schemes Of policy can never make me tremble.

MARQUIS.

Whether the Infant loves her--whether we Have something worse to fear from him,-- are things Worthy our deep attention. To these points Our strictest vigilance must be directed.

KING.

You must be pledge for him.

MARQUIS.

And if the king Esteem me capable of such a task, I must entreat it be intrusted to me Wholly without conditions.

KING.

So it shall.

MARQUIS.

That in the steps which I may think required, I may be thwarted by no coadjutors, Whatever name they bear.

KING.

I pledge my word You shall not. You have proved my guardian angel. How many thanks I owe you for this service!

[LERMA enters--the KING to him. How did you leave the queen?

LERMA.

But scarce recovered From her deep swoon.

[He looks at the MARQUIS doubtfully, and exit. MARQUIS (to the KING, after a pause).

One caution yet seems needful.

The prince may be advised of our design, For he has many faithful friends in Ghent, And may have partisans among the rebels. Fear may incite to desperate resolves; Therefore I counsel that some speedy means Be taken to prevent this fatal chance.

KING.

You are quite right--but how?

MARQUIS.

Your majesty May sign a secret warrant of arrest And place it in my hands, to be employed, As may seem needful, in the hour of danger.

[The KING appears thoughtful.

This step must be a most profound state secret Until----

KING (going to his desk and writing the warrant of arrest). The kingdom is at stake, and now The pressing danger sanctions urgent measures.

Here marquis! I need scarcely say--use prudence.

MARQUIS (taking the warrant). 'Tis only for the last extremity.

KING (laying his hand on the shoulder of the MARQUIS). Go! Go, dear marquis! Give this bosom peace, And bring back slumber to my sleepless pillow. [Exeunt at different sides.

SCENE XIII.

A Gallery.

CARLOS entering in extreme agitation, COUNT LERMA meeting him.

CARLOS.

I have been seeking you.

LERMA.

And I your highness.

CARLOS.

For heaven's sake is it true?

LERMA.

What do you mean?

CARLOS.

That the king drew his dagger, and that she Was borne, all bathed in blood, from the apartment? Now answer me, by all that's sacred; say, What am I to believe? What truth is in it?

LERMA.

She fainted, and so grazed her skin in falling That is the whole.

CARLOS.

Is there no further danger? Count, answer on your honor.

LERMA.

For the queen No further danger; for yourself, there's much!

CARLOS.

None for my mother. Then, kind Heaven, I thank thee. A dreadful rumor reached me that the king Raved against child and mother, and that some Dire secret was discovered.

LERMA.

And the last May possibly be true.

CARLOS.

Be true! What mean you?

LERMA.

One warning have I given you, prince, already, And that to-day, but you despised it; now Perhaps you'll profit better by a second.

CARLOS.

Explain yourself.

LERMA.

If I mistake not, prince, A few days since I noticed in your hands An azure-blue portfolio, worked in velvet And chased with gold.

CARLOS (with anxiety). Yes, I had such a one.

LERMA.

And on the cover, if I recollect, a portrait Set in pearls?

CARLOS.

'Tis right; go on.

LERMA.

I entered the king's chamber on a sudden,

And in his hands I marked that same portfolio, The Marquis Posa standing by his side.

CARLOS (after a short silence of astonishment, hastily). 'Tis false!

LERMA (warmly). Then I'm a traitor!

CARLOS (looking steadfastly at him). That you are!

LERMA.

Well, I forgive you.

CARLOS (paces the apartment in extreme agitation, at length stands still before him).

Has he injured thee?

What have our guiltless ties of friendship done, That with a demon's zeal thou triest to rend them?

LERMA.

Prince, I respect the grief which renders you So far unjust.

CARLOS.

Heaven shield me from suspicion!

LERMA.

And I remember, too, the king's own words. Just as I entered he addressed the marquis:

"How many thanks I owe you for this news."

CARLOS.

Oh, say no more!

LERMA.

Duke Alva is disgraced!

The great seal taken from the Prince Ruy Gomez, And given to the marquis.

CARLOS (lost in deep thought). And from me Has he concealed all this? And why from me?

LERMA.

As minister all-powerful, the court

Looks on him now--as favorite unrivalled!

CARLOS.

He loved me--loved me greatly: I was dear As his own soul is to him. That I know--

Of that I've had a thousand proofs. But should The happiness of millions yield to one?

Must not his country dearer to him prove Than Carlos? One friend only is too few For his capacious heart. And not enough Is Carlos' happiness to engross his love. He offers me a sacrifice to virtue; And shall I murmur at him? Now 'tis certain I have forever lost him.

[He steps aside and covers his face.

LERMA.

Dearest prince!

How can I serve you?

CARLOS (without looking at him). Get you to the king;

Go and betray me. I have naught to give.

LERMA.

Will you then stay and brave the ill that follows?

CARLOS (leans on a balustrade and looks forward with a vacant gaze). I've lost him now, and I am destitute!

LERMA (approaching him with sympathizing emotion). And will you not consult your safety, prince?

CARLOS.

My safety! Generous man!

LERMA:

And is there, then, No other person you should tremble for?

CARLOS (starts up).

Heavens! you remind me now. Alas! My mother! The letter that I gave him--first refused-- Then after, gave him!

[He paces backwards and forwards with agitation, wringing his hands.

Has she then deserved This blow from him? He should have spared her, Lerma.

[In a hasty, determined tone.

But I must see her--warn her of her danger-- I must prepare her, Lerma, dearest Lerma! Whom shall I send? Have I no friend remaining? Yes! Heaven be praised! I still have one; and now The worst is over.

[Exit quickly.

LEEMA (follows, and calls after him). Whither, whither, prince?

SCENE XIV.

The QUEEN, ALVA, DOMINGO.

ALVA.

If we may be permitted, gracious queen----

QUEEN.

What are your wishes?

DOMINGO.

A most true regard For your high majesty forbids us now To watch in careless silence an event Pregnant with danger to your royal safety.

ALVA.

We hasten, by a kind and timely warning, To counteract a plot that's laid against you.

DOMINGO.

And our warm zeal, and our best services, To lay before your feet, most gracious queen!

QUEEN

(looking at them with astonishment). Most reverend sir, and you, my noble duke, You much surprise me. Such sincere attachment, In truth, I had not hoped for from Domingo, Nor from Duke Alva. Much I value it.

A plot you mention, menacing my safety-- Dare I inquire by whom----

ALVA.

You will beware a certain Marquis Posa He has of late been secretly employed In the king's service.

QUEEN.

With delight I hear The king has made so excellent a choice. Report, long since, has spoken of the marquis As a deserving, great, and virtuous man-- The royal grace was ne'er so well bestowed!

DOMINGO.

So well bestowed! We think far otherwise.

ALVA.

It is no secret now, for what designs This man has been employed.

QUEEN.

How! What designs?

You put my expectation on the rack.

DOMINGO.

How long is it since last your majesty Opened your casket?

QUEEN.

Why do you inquire?

DOMINGO.

Did you not miss some articles of value?

QUEEN.

Why these suspicions? What I missed was then Known to the court! But what of Marquis Posa? Say, what connection has all this with him?

ALVA.

The closest, please your majesty--the prince Has lost some papers of importance;

And they were seen this morning with the king After the marquis had an audience of him.

QUEEN

(after some consideration).

This news is strange indeed—inexplicablem To find a foe where I could ne'er have dreamed it, And two warm friends I knew not I possessed!

[Fixing her eyes steadfastly upon them. And, to speak truth, I had well nigh imputed To you the wicked turn my husband served me.

ALVA.

To us!

QUEEN.

To you yourselves!

DOMINGO.

To me! Duke Alva!

QUEEN (her eyes still fastened on them). I am glad to be so timely made aware Of my rash judgment--else had I resolved This very day to beg his majesty Would bring me face to face with my accusers. But I'm contented now. I can appeal To the Duke Alva for his testimony.

ALVA.

For mine? You would not sure do that!

QUEEN.

Why not?

ALVA.

'Twould counteract the services we might Render in secret to you.

QUEEN.

How! in secret? [With stern dignity.

I fain would know what secret projects, duke, Your sovereign's spouse can have to form with you, Or, priest! with you--her husband should not know? Think you that I am innocent or guilty?

DOMINGO.

Strange question!

ALVA.

Should the monarch prove unjust-- And at this time----

QUEEN.

Then I must wait for justice Until it come--and they are happiest far Whose consciences may calmly wait their right.

[Bows to them and exit. DOMINGO and ALVA exeunt on the opposite side.

SCENE XV.

Chamber Of PRINCESS EBOLI.

PRINCESS EBOLI. CARLOS immediately after.

EBOLI.

Is it then true--the strange intelligence, That fills the court with wonder?

CARLOS (enters). Do not fear Princess! I shall be gentle as a child.

EBOLI.

Prince, this intrusion!

CARLOS.

Are you angry still? Offended still with me----

EBOLI.

Prince!

CARLOS (earnestly). Are you angry?

I pray you answer me.

EBOLI.

What can this mean?

You seem, prince, to forget--what would you with me?

CARLOS (seizing her hand with warmth). Dear maiden! Can you hate eternally?

Can injured love ne'er pardon?

EBOLI (disengaging herself). Prince! of what Would you remind me?

CARLOS.

Of your kindness, dearest!

And of my deep ingratitude. Alas, Too well I know it! deeply have I wronged thee-- Wounded thy tender heart, and from thine eyes, Thine angel eyes, wrung precious tears, sweet maid! But ah! 'tis not repentance leads me hither.

EBOLI.

Prince! leave me--I----

CARLOS.

I come to thee, because Thou art a maid of gentle soul—because I trust thy heart--thy kind and tender heart. Think, dearest maiden! think, I have no friend, No friend but thee, in all this wretched world-- Thou who wert once so kind wilt not forever Hate me, nor will thy anger prove eternal.

EBOLI (turning away her face).

O cease! No more! for heaven's sake! leave me, prince.

CARLOS.

Let me remind thee of those golden hours-- Let me remind thee of thy love, sweet maid-- That love which I so basely have offended!

Oh, let me now appear to thee again As once I was--and as thy heart portrayed me. Yet once again, once only, place my image, As in days past, before thy tender soul,

And to that idol make a sacrifice Thou canst not make to me.

EBOLI.

Oh, Carlos, cease!

Too cruelly thou sportest with my feelings!

CARLOS.

Be nobler than thy sex! Forgive an insult!

Do what no woman e'er has done before thee, And what no woman, after thee, can equal.

I ask of thee an unexampled favor. Grant me--upon my knees I ask of thee Grant me two moments with the queen, my mother! [He casts himself at her feet.

SCENE XVI.

The former. MARQUIS POSA rushes in; behind him two Officers of the Queen's Guard.

MARQUIS (breathless and agitated, rushing between CARLOS and the PRINCESS).

Say, what has he confessed? Believe him not!

CARLOS (still on his knees, with loud voice). By all that's holy----

MARQUIS (interrupting him with vehemence). He is mad! He raves!

Oh, listen to him not!

CARLOS (louder and more urgent). It is a question Of life and death; conduct me to her straight.

MARQUIS (dragging the PRINCESS from him by force). You die, if you but listen.

[To one of the officers, showing an order. Count of Cordova!

In the king's name, Prince Carlos is your prisoner.

[CARLOS stands bewildered. The PRINCESS utters a cry of horror, and tries to escape. The officers are astounded. A long and deep pause ensues. The MARQUIS trembles violently, and with difficulty preserves his composure.

[To the PRINCE.

I beg your sword--The Princess Eboli Remains---- [To the officers.

And you, on peril of your lives, Let no one with his highness speak--no person-- Not e'en yourselves.

[He whispers a few words to one officer, then turns to the other. I hasten, instantly, To cast myself before our monarch's feet, And justify this step---- [To the PRINCE. And prince! for you-- Expect me in an hour.

[CARLOS permits himself to be led away without any signs of consciousness, except that in passing he casts a languid, dying look on the MARQUIS. The PRINCESS endeavors again to escape; the MARQUIS pulls her back by the arm.

SCENE XVII.

PRINCESS EBOLI, MARQUIS POSA. EBOLI.

For Heaven's sake let me leave this place----

MARQUIS (leads her forward with dreadful earnestness).

Thou wretch!

What has he said to thee?

EBOLI.

Oh, leave me! Nothing.

MARQUIS (with earnestness; holding her back by force). How much has he imparted to thee? Here No way is left thee to escape. To none In this world shalt thou ever tell it.

EBOLI (looking at him with terror).

Heavens! What would you do? Would you then murder me?

MARQUIS (drawing a dagger). Yes, that is my resolve. Be speedy!

EBOLI.

Mercy!

What have I then committed?

MARQUIS (looking towards heaven, points the dagger to her breast). Still there's time-- The poison has not issued from these lips. Dash but the bowl to atoms, all remains Still as before! The destinies of Spain Against a woman's life!

[Remains doubtingly in this position.

EBOLI (having sunk down beside him, looks in his face).

Do not delay-- Why do you hesitate? I beg no mercy-- I have deserved to die, and I am ready.

MARQUIS (letting his hand drop slowly--after some reflection). It were as cowardly as barbarous.

No! God be praised! another way is left.

[He lets the dagger fall and hurries out. The PRINCESS hastens out through another door.

SCENE XVIII.

A Chamber of the QUEEN.

The QUEEN to the COUNTESS FUENTES.

What means this noisy tumult in the palace? Each breath to-day alarms me! Countess! see what it portends, and hasten back with speed.

[Exit COUNTESS FUENTES--the PRINCESS EBOLI rushes in.

SCENE XIX.

The QUEEN, PRINCESS EBOLI.

EBOLI (breathless, pale, and wild, falls before the QUEEN). Help! Help! O Queen! he's seized!

QUEEN.

Who?

EBOLI.

He's arrested By the king's orders given to Marquis Posa.

QUEEN.

Who is arrested? Who?

EBOLI.

The prince!

QUEEN.

Thou ravest

EBOLI.

This moment they are leading him away.

QUEEN.

And who arrested him?

EBOLI.

The Marquis Posa.

QUEEN.

Then heaven be praised! it was the marquis seized him!

EBOLI.

Can you speak thus, and with such tranquil mien? Oh, heavens! you do not know--you cannot think----

QUEEN.

The cause of his arrest! some trifling error, Doubtless arising from his headlong youth!

EBOLI.

No! no! I know far better. No, my queen! Remorseless treachery! There's no help for him. He dies!

QUEEN.

He dies!

EBOLI.

And I'm his murderer!

QUEEN.

What! Dies? Thou ravest! Think what thou art saying?

EBOLI.

And wherefore--wherefore dies he? Had I known That it would come to this!

QUEEN (takes her affectionately by the hand). Oh, dearest princess, Your senses are distracted, but collect Your wandering spirits, and relate to me More calmly, not in images of horror That fright my inmost soul, whate'er you know! Say, what has happened?

EBOLI.

Oh, display not, queen, Such heavenly condescension! Like hot flames This kindness sears my conscience. I'm not worthy To view thy purity with eyes profane.

Oh, crush the wretch, who, agonized by shame, Remorse, and self-reproach writhes at thy feet!

QUEEN.

Unhappy woman! Say, what is thy guilt?

EBOLI.

Angel of light! Sweet saint! thou little knowest The demon who has won thy loving smiles.

Know her to-day; I was the wretched thief Who plundered thee.

QUEEN.

What! Thou?

165

EBOLI.

And gave thy letters Up to the king?

QUEEN.

What! Thou?

EBOLI.

And dared accuse thee!

QUEEN.

Thou! Couldst thou this?

EBOLI.

Revenge and madness--love-- I hated thee, and loved the prince!

QUEEN.

And did

His love so prompt thee?

QUEEN.

And who arrested him?

EBOLI.

I had owned my love, But met with no return.

QUEEN

(after a pause). Now all's explained!

Rise up!--you loved him--I have pardoned you

I have forgotten all. Now, princess, rise. [Holding out her hand to the PRINCESS.

EBOLI.

No, no; a foul confession still remains. I will not rise, great queen, till I----

QUEEN.

Then speak!

What have I yet to hear?

EBOLI.

The king! Seduction!

Oh, now you turn away. And in your eyes I read abhorrence. Yes; of that foul crime I charged you with, I have myself been guilty.

[She presses her burning face to the ground. Exit QUEEN. A long pause. The COUNTESS OLIVAREZ, after some minutes, comes out of the cabinet, into which the QUEEN entered, and finds the PRINCESS still lying in the above posture. She approaches in silence. On hearing a noise, the latter looks up and becomes like a mad person when she misses the QUEEN.

SCENE XX.

PRINCESS EBOLI, COUNTESS OLIVAREZ. EBOLI.

Heavens! she has left me. I am now undone!

OLIVAREZ (approaching her). My princess--Eboli!

EBOLI.

I know your business, Duchess, and you come hither from the queen, To speak my sentence to me; do it quickly.

OLIVAREZ.

I am commanded by your majesty To take your cross and key.

EBOLI (takes from her breast a golden cross, and gives it to the UCHESS). And but once more May I not kiss my gracious sovereign's hand?

OLIVAREZ.

In holy Mary's convent shall you learn Your fate, princess.

EBOLI (with a flood of tears).

Alas! then I no more Shall ever see the queen.

OLIVAREZ (embraces her with her face turned away). Princess, farewell.

[She goes hastily away. The PRINCESS follows her as far as the door of the cabinet, which is immediately locked after the DUCHESS. She remains a few minutes silent and motionless on her knees before it. She then rises and hastens away, covering her face.

SCENE XXI.

QUEEN, MARQUIS POSA. QUEEN.

Ah, marquis, I am glad you're come at last!

MARQUIS (pale, with a disturbed countenance and trembling voice, in solemn, deep agitation, during the whole scene). And is your majesty alone? Can none Within the adjoining chamber overhear us?

QUEEN.

No one! But why? What news would you impart? [Looking at him closely, and drawing back alarmed.

And what has wrought this change in you? Speak, marquis, You make me tremble--all your features seem So marked with death!

MARQUIS.

You know, perhaps, already.

QUEEN.

That Carlos is arrested--and they add, By you! Is it then true? From no one else Would I believe it but yourself.

MARQUIS.

'Tis true.

QUEEN.

By you?

MARQUIS.

By me?

QUEEN (looks at him for some time doubtingly). I still respect your actions E'en when I comprehend them not. In this Pardon a timid woman! I much fear You play a dangerous game.

MARQUIS.

And I have lost it.

QUEEN.

Merciful heaven!

MARQUIS.

Queen, fear not! He is safe, But I am lost myself.

QUEEN.

What do I hear?

MARQUIS.

Who bade me hazard all on one chance throw? All? And with rash, foolhardy confidence, Sport with the power of heaven? Of bounded mind, Man, who is not omniscient, must not dare To guide the helm of destiny. 'Tis just!

But why these thoughts of self. This hour is precious As life can be to man: and who can tell Whether the parsimonious hand of fate May not have measured my last drops of life.

QUEEN.

The hand of fate! What means this solemn tone? I understand these words not--but I shudder.

MARQUIS.

He's saved! no matter at what price--he's saved! But only for to-day--a few short hours Are his. Oh, let him husband them! This night The prince must leave Madrid.

QUEEN.

This very night?

MARQUIS.

All measures are prepared. The post will meet him At the Carthusian convent, which has served So long as an asylum to our friendship. Here will he find, in letters of exchange, All in the world that fortune gifts me with.

Should more be wanting, you must e'en supply it.

In truth, I have within my heart full much To unburden to my Carlos--it may chance I shall want leisure now to tell him all In person--but this evening you will see him, And therefore I address myself to you.

QUEEN.

Oh, for my peace of mind, dear marquis, speak! Explain yourself more clearly! Do not use This dark, and fearful, and mysterious language! Say, what has happened?

MARQUIS.

I have yet one thing, A matter of importance on my mind: In your hands I deposit it. My lot Was such as few indeed have e'er enjoyed-- I loved a prince's son. My heart to one-- To that one object given.--embraced the world! I have created in my Carlos' soul, A paradise for millions! Oh, my dream Was lovely! But the will of Providence Has summoned me away, before my hour, From this my beauteous work. His Roderigo Soon shall be his no more, and friendship's claim Will be transferred to love. Here, therefore, here, Upon this sacred altar--on the heart Of his loved queen--I lay my last bequest A precious legacy--he'll find it here, When I shall be no more.

[He turns away, his voice choked with grief.

QUEEN.

This is the language Of a dying man--it surely emanates But from your blood's excitement--or does sense Lie hidden in your language?

MARQUIS

(Has endeavored to collect himself, and continues in a solemn voice). Tell the prince, That he must ever bear in mind the oath We swore, in past enthusiastic days, Upon the sacred host. I have kept mine-- I'm true to him till death--'tis now his turn----

QUEEN.

Till death?

MARQUIS.

Oh, bid him realize the dream, The glowing vision which our friendship painted, Of a new-perfect realm! And let him lay The first hand on the rude, unshapened stone. Whether he fail or prosper--all alike-- Let him commence the work. When centuries Have rolled away shall Providence again Raise to the throne a princely youth like him, And animate again a favorite son Whose breast shall burn with like enthusiasm. Tell him, in manhood, he must still revere The dreams of early youth, nor ope the heart Of heaven's all-tender flower to canker-worms Of boasted reason,--nor be led astray When, by the wisdom of the dust, he hears Enthusiasm, heavenly-born, blasphemed.

I have already told him.

QUEEN.

Whither, marquis? Whither does all this tend?

MARQUIS.

And tell him further, I lay upon his soul the happiness Of man--that with my dying breath I claim, Demand it of him--and with justest title. I had designed a new, a glorious morn, To waken in these kingdoms: for to me Philip had opened all his inmost heart--

Called me his son--bestowed his seals upon me-- And Alva was no more his counsellor.

[He pauses, and looks at the QUEEN for a few moments in silence. You weep! I know those tears, beloved soul!

Oh, they are tears of joy!--but it is past-- Forever past! Carlos or I? The choice Was prompt and fearful. One of us must perish! And I will be that one. Oh, ask no more!

QUEEN.

Now, now, at last, I comprehend your meaning, Unhappy man! What have you done?

MARQUIS.

Cut off Two transient hours of evening to secure A long, bright summer-day! I now give up The king forever. What were I to the king?

In such cold soil no rose of mine could bloom; In my great friend must Europe's fortune ripen. Spain I bequeath to him, still bathed in blood From Philip's iron hand. But woe to him, Woe to us both, if I have chosen wrong! But no--oh, no! I know my Carlos better--

'Twill never come to pass!--for this, my queen, You stand my surety. [After a silence. Yes! I saw his love In its first blossom--saw his fatal passion Take root in his young heart. I had full power To check it; but I did not. The attachment Which seemed to me not guilty, I still nourished. The world may censure me, but I repent not, Nor does my heart accuse me. I saw life Where death appeared to others. In a flame So hopeless I discerned hope's golden beam. I wished to lead him to the excellent-- To exalt him to the highest point of beauty. Mortality denied a model to me, And language, words. Then did I bend his views To this point only--and my whole endeavor Was to explain to him his love.

QUEEN.

Your friend, Marquis! so wholly occupied your mind, That for his cause you quite forgot my own-- Could you suppose that I had thrown aside All woman's weaknesses, that you could dare Make me his angel, and confide alone In virtue for his armor? You forget What risks this heart must run, when we ennoble Passion with such a beauteous name as this.

MARQUIS.

Yes, in all other women--but in one, One only, 'tis not so. For you, I swear it.

And should you blush to indulge the pure desire To call heroic virtue into life?

Can it affect King Philip, that his works Of noblest art, in the Escurial, raise Immortal longings in the painter's soul, Who stands entranced before them? Do the sounds That slumber in the lute, belong alone To him who buys the chords? With ear unmoved He may preserve his treasure:--he has bought The wretched right to shiver it to atoms, But not the power to wake its silver tones, Or, in the magic of its sounds, dissolve.

Truth is created for the sage, as beautyIs for the feeling heart. They own each other. And this belief, no coward prejudice shall make me e'er disclaim. Then promise, queen, That you will ever love him. That false shame,

Or fancied dignity, shall never make you Yield to the voice of base dissimulation:--

That you will love him still, unchanged, forever. Promise me this, oh, queen! Here solemnly Say, do you promise?

QUEEN.

That my heart alone Shall ever vindicate my love, I promise----

MARQUIS (drawing his hand back). Now I die satisfied--my work is done.

[He bows to the QUEEN, and is about to go.

QUEEN (follows him with her eyes in silence). You are then going, marquis, and have not Told me how soon--and when--we meet again?

MARQUIS (comes back once more, his face turned away). Yes, we shall surely meet again!

QUEEN.

Now, Posa, I understand you. Why have you done this?

MARQUIS.

Carlos or I myself!

QUEEN.

No! no! you rush Headlong into a deed you deem, sublime. Do not deceive yourself: I know you well: Long have you thirsted for it. If your pride But have its fill, what matters it to you Though thousand hearts should break. Oh! now, at length, I comprehend your feelings--'tis the love Of admiration which has won your heart----

MARQUIS

(Surprised, aside). No! I was not prepared for this----

QUEEN

(After a pause). Oh, marquis!

Is there no hope of preservation?

MARQUIS.

None.

QUEEN.

None? Oh, consider well! None possible! Not e'en by me?

MARQUIS.

Not even, queen, by thee.

QUEEN.

You but half know me--I have courage, marquis----

MARQUIS.

I know it----

QUEEN.

And no means of safety?

MARQUIS.

None

QUEEN

(Turning away and covering her face). Go! Never more shall I respect a man----

MARQUIS

(Casts himself on his knees before her in evident emotion). O queen! O heaven! how lovely still is life!

[He starts up and rushes out. The QUEEN retires into her cabinet.

SCENE XXII.

DUKE ALVA and DOMINGO walking up and down in silence and separately. COUNT LERMA comes out of the KING's cabinet, and afterwards DON RAYMOND OF TAXIS, the Postmaster-General.

LERMA.

Has not the marquis yet appeared?

ALVA.

Not yet.

[LERMA about to re-enter the cabinet. TAXIS (enters).

Count Lerma! Pray announce me to the king?

LERMA.

His majesty cannot be seen.

TAXIS.

But say

That I must see him; that my business is Of urgent import to his majesty.

Make haste--it will admit of no delay. [LERMA enters the cabinet.

ALVA.

Dear Taxis, you must learn a little patience-- You cannot see the king.

TAXIS.

Not see him! Why?

ALVA.

You should have been considerate, and procured Permission from the Marquis Posa first--Who keeps both son and father in confinement.

TAXIS.

The Marquis Posa! Right--that is the man From whom I bring this letter.

ALVA.

Ah! What letter?

TAXIS.

A letter to be forwarded to Brussels.

ALVA (attentively). To Brussels?

TAXIS.

And I bring it to the king.

ALVA.

Indeed! To Brussels! Heard you that, Domingo?

DOMINGO (joining them). Full of suspicion!

TAXIS.

And with anxious mien, And deep embarrassment he gave it to me.

DOMINGO.

Embarrassment! To whom is it directed?

TAXIS.

The Prince of Orange and Nassau.

ALVA.

To William!

There's treason here, Domingo!

DOMINGO.

Nothing less!

In truth this letter must, without delay, Be laid before the king. A noble service You render, worthy man--to be so firm In the discharge of duty.

TAXIS.

Reverend sir! 'Tis but my duty.

ALVA.

But you do it well.

LERMA (coming out of the cabinet, addressing TAXIS). The king will see you.

[TAXIS goes in.

Is the marquis come?

DOMINGO.

He has been sought for everywhere.

ALVA.

'Tis strange!

The prince is a state prisoner! And the king Knows not the reason why!

DOMINGO.

He never came To explain the business here.

ALVA.

What says the king?

LERMA.

The king spoke not a word. [A noise in the cabinet.

ALVA.

What noise is that?

TAXIS

(Coming out of the cabinet). Count Lerma! [Both enter.

ALVA (to DOMINGO).

What so deeply can engage them?

DOMINGO.

That look of fear! This intercepted letter! It augurs nothing good.

ALVA.

He sends for Lerma!

Yet he must know full well that you and I Are both in waiting.

DOMINGO.

Ah! our day is over!

ALVA.

And am I not the same to whom these doors Flew open once? But, ah! how changed is all Around me and how strange!

[DOMINGO approaches the cabinet door softly, and remains listening before it.

ALVA (after a pause).

Hark! All is still And silent as the grave!' I hear them breathe.

DOMINGO.

The double tapestry absorbs the sounds!

ALVA.

Away! there's some one coming. All appears So solemn and so still--as if this instant

Some deep momentous question were decided.

SCENE XXIII.

The PRINCE OF PARMA, the DUKES OF FERIA and MEDINA SIDONIA, with other GRANDEES enter--the preceding.

PARMA.

Say, can we see the king?

ALVA.

No!

PARMA.

Who is with him?

FERIA.

The Marquis Posa, doubtless?

ALVA.

Every instant He is expected here.

PARMA.

This moment we Arrive from Saragossa. Through Madrid Terror prevails! Is the announcement true?

Domingo. Alas, too true!

FERIA.

That he has been arrested By the marquis!

ALVA.

Yes.

PARMA.

And wherefore? What's the cause?

ALVA.

Wherefore? That no one knows, except the king And Marquis Posa.

PARMA.

And without the warrant Of the assembled Cortes of the Realm?

FERIA.

That man shall suffer, who has lent a hand To infringe the nation's rights.

ALVA.

And so say I!

MEDINA SIDONIA.

And I!

THE OTHER GRANDEES.

And all of us!

ALVA.

Who'll follow me Into the cabinet? I'll throw myself Before the monarch's feet.

LERMA (rushing out of the cabinet). The Duke of Alva!

DOMINGO.

Then God be praised at last!

LERMA.

When Marquis Posa Comes, say the king's engaged and he'll be sent for.

DOMINGO (to LERMA; all the others having gathered round him, full of anxious expectation).

Count! What has happened? You are pale as death!

LERMA (hastening away). Fell villany!

PARMA and FERIA.

What! what!

MEDINA SIDONIA.

How is the king?

DOMINGO (at the same time). Fell villany! Explain----

LERMA.

The king shed tears!

DOMINGO.

Shed tears!

ALL (together with astonishment).

The king shed tears!

[The bell rings in the cabinet, COUNT LERMA hastens in.

DOMINGO.

Count, yet one word.

Pardon! He's gone! We're fettered in amazement.

SCENE XXIV.

PRINCESS EBOLI, FERIA, MEDINA SIDONIA, PARMA,

DOMINGO, and other grandees.

EBOLI (hurriedly and distractedly).

Where is the king? Where? I must speak with him.

[To FERIA.

Conduct me to him, duke!

FERIA.

The monarch is Engaged in urgent business. No one now Can be admitted.

EBOLI.

Has he signed, as yet, The fatal sentence? He has been deceived.

DOMINGO (giving her a significant look at a distance). The Princess Eboli!

EBOLI (going to him).

What! you here, priest?

The very man I want! You can confirm My testimony!

[She seizes his hand and would drag him into the cabinet.

DOMINGO.

I? You rave, princess!

FERIA.

Hold back. The king cannot attend you now.

EBOLI.

But he must hear me; he must hear the truth The truth, were he ten times a deity.

EBOLI.

Man, tremble at the anger of thy idol. I have naught left to hazard.

[Attempts to enter the cabinet; ALVA rushes out, his eyes sparkling, triumph in his gait. He hastens to DOMINGO, and embraces him.

ALVA.

Let each church Resound with high To Dennis. Victory At length is ours.

DOMINGO.

What! Ours?

ALVA (to DOMINGO and the other GRANDEES).

Now to the king.

You shall hereafter hear the sequel from me.

ACT V.

SCENE I.

A chamber in the royal palace, separated from a large fore-court by an iron-barred gate. Sentinels walking up and down. CARLOS sitting at a table, with his head leaning forward on his arms, as if he were asleep. In the background of the chamber are some officers, confined with him. The MARQUIS POSA enters, unobserved by him, and whispers to the officers, who immediately withdraw. He himself steps close up to CARLOS, and looks at him for a few minutes in silent sorrow. At last he makes a motion which awakens him out of his stupor. CARLOS rises, and seeing the MARQUIS, starts back. He regards him for some time with fixed eyes, and draws his hand over his forehead as if he wished to recollect something.

MARQUIS.

Carlos! 'tie I.

CARLOS (gives him his hand). Comest thou to me again?

'Tis friendly of thee, truly.

MARQUIS.

Here I thought Thou mightest need a friend.

CARLOS.

Indeed! was that Thy real thought? Oh, joy unspeakable! Right well I knew thou still wert true to me.

MARQUIS.

I have deserved this from thee.

CARLOS.

Hast thou not?

And now we understand each other fully, It joys my heart. This kindness, this forbearance Becomes our noble souls. For should there be One rash, unjust demand amongst my wishes, Wouldst thou, for that, refuse me what was just? Virtue I know may often be severe, But never is she cruel and inhuman.

Oh! it hath cost thee much; full well I know How thy kind heart with bitter anguish bled As thy hands decked the victim for the altar.

MARQUIS.

What meanest thou, Carlos?

CARLOS.

Thou, thyself, wilt now

Fulfil the joyous course I should have run. Thou wilt bestow on Spain those golden days She might have hoped in vain to win from me. I'm lost, forever lost; thou saw'st it clearly.

This fatal love has scattered, and forever, All the bright, early blossoms of my mind. To all the great, exalted hopes I'm dead.

Chance led thee to the king--or Providence,-- It cost thee but my secret--and at once He was thine own--thou may'st become his angel: But I am lost, though Spain perhaps may flourish. Well, there is nothing to condemn, if not My own mad blindness. Oh, I should have known That thou art no less great than tender-hearted.

MARQUIS.

No! I foresaw not, I considered not That friendship's generous heart would lead thee on Beyond my worldly prudence. I have erred, My fabric's shattered--I forgot thy heart.

CARLOS.

Yet, if it had been possible to spare Her fate--oh, how intensely I had thanked thee! Could I not bear the burden by myself?

And why must she be made a second victim? But now no more, I'll spare thee this reproach.

What is the queen to thee? Say, dost thou love her? Could thy exalted virtue e'er consult The petty interests of my wretched passion? Oh, pardon me! I was unjust----

MARQUIS.

Thou art so!

But not for this reproach. Deserved I one, I merit all--and then I should not stand Before you as I do.

[He takes out his portfolio. I have some letters To give you back of those you trusted to me.

CARLOS

(Looks first at the letters, then at the MARQUIS, in astonishment).

How!

I return them now because they may Prove safer in thy custody than mine.

CARLOS.

What meanest thou? Has his majesty not read them? Have they not been before him?

MARQUIS.

What, these letters!

CARLOS.

Thou didst not show them all, then?

MARQUIS.

Who has said That ever I showed one?

CARLOS

(Astonished). Can it be so?

Count Lerma----

MARQUIS.

He! he told thee so! Now all

Is clear as day. But who could have foreseen it? Lerma! Oh, no, he hath not learned to lie. 'Tis true, the king has all the other letters.

CARLOS

(Looks at him long with speechless astonishment). But wherefore am I here?

For caution's sake, Lest thou should chance, a second time, to make An Eboli thy confidant.

CARLOS (as if waking from a dream). Ha! Now

I see it all--all is explained.

MARQUIS (goes to the door). Who's there?

SCENE II.

DUKE ALVA. The former.

ALVA (approaching the PRINCE with respect, but turning his back on the MARQUIS during the whole scene).

Prince, you are free. Deputed by the king I come to tell you so.

[CARLOS looks at the MARQUIS with astonishment. General silence.

And I, in truth, Am fortunate to have this honor first----

CARLOS

(Looking at both with extreme amazement, after a pause, to the DUKE).

I am imprisoned, duke, and set at freedom, Unconscious of the cause of one or other.

ALVA.

As far as I know, prince, 'twas through an error, To which the king was driven by a traitor.

CARLOS.

Then am I here by order of the king?

ALVA.

Yes, through an error of his majesty.

CARLOS.

That gives me pain, indeed. But when the king Commits an error, 'twould beseem the king, Methinks, to remedy the fault in person.

I am Don Philip's son--and curious eyes And slanderous looks are on me. What the king Hath done from sense of duty ne'er will I Appear to owe to your considerate favor.

I am prepared to appear before the Cortes, And will not take my sword from such a hand.

ALVA.

The king will never hesitate to grant Your highness a request so just. Permit That I conduct you to him.

CARLOS.

Here I stay Until the king or all Madrid shall come To lead me from my prison. Take my answer.

[ALVA withdraws. He is still seen for some time lingering in the court and giving orders to the guards.

SCENE III.

CARLOS and MARQUIS POSA.

CARLOS (after the departure of the DUKE, full of expectation and astonishment, to the MARQUIS).

What means all this? Inform me, Roderigo-- Art thou not, then, the minister?

MARQUIS.

I was, As thou canst well perceive---- [Going to him with great emotion. O Carlos! Now I have succeeded--yes--it is accomplished-- 'Tis over now--Omnipotence be praised, To whom I owe success.

CARLOS.

Success! What mean you? Thy words perplex me.

MARQUIS (takes his hand). Carlos! thou art saved--

Art free--but I----

[He stops short.

CARLOS.

But thou----

MARQUIS.

Thus to my breast I press thee now, with friendship's fullest right, A right I've bought with all I hold most dear.

How great, how lovely, Carlos, is this moment Of self-approving joy?

CARLOS.

What sudden change I mark upon thy features! Proudly now Thy bosom heaves, thine eyes dart vivid fire!

MARQUIS.

We must say farewell, Carlos! Tremble 'not, But be a man! And what thou more shalt hear, Promise me, not by unavailing sorrow, Unworthy of great souls, to aggravate The pangs of parting. I am lost to thee, Carlos, for many years--fools say forever.

[CARLOS withdraws his hand, but makes no reply. Be thou a man: I've reckoned much on thee-- I have not even shunned to pass with thee This awful hour--which men, in words of fear, Have termed the final one. I own it, Carlos, I joy to pass it thus. Come let us sit-- I feel myself grown weary and exhausted.

[He approaches CARLOS, who is in a lifeless stupor, and allows himself to be involuntarily drawn down by him. Where art thou? No reply! I must be brief. Upon the day that followed our last meeting At the Carthusian monastery the king Called me before him. What ensued thou knowest, And all Madrid. Thou hast not heard, however, Thy secret even then had reached his ears-- That letters in the queen's possession found Had testified against thee. This I learned From his own lips--I was his confidant.

[He pauses for CARLOS' answer, but he still remains silent.

Yes, Carlos, with my lips I broke my faith-- Guided the plot myself that worked thy ruin.

Thy deed spoke trumpet-tongued; to clear thee fully 'Twas now too late: to frustrate his revenge Was all that now remained for me; and so I made myself thy enemy to-serve thee With fuller power--dost thou not hear me, Carlos,

CARLOS.

Go on! go on! I hear thee.

MARQUIS.

To this point I'm guiltless. But the unaccustomed beams Of royal favor dazzled me. The rumor, As I had well foreseen, soon reached thine ears But by mistaken delicacy led, And blinded by my vain desire to end My enterprise alone, I kept concealed From friendship's ear my hazardous design. This was my fatal error! Here I failed!

I know it. My self-confidence was madness. Pardon that confidence--'twas founded, Carlos, Upon our friendship's everlasting base.

[He pauses. CARLOS passes from torpid silence to violent agitation.

That which I feared befell. Unreal dangers Alarmed your mind. The bleeding queen--the tumult Within the palace--Lerma's interference-- And, last of all, my own mysterious silence, Conspired to overwhelm thy heart with wonder. Thou wavered'st, thought'st me lost; but far too noble To doubt thy friend's integrity, thy soul Clothed his defection with a robe of honor, Nor judged him faithless till it found a motive To screen and justify his breach of faith.

Forsaken by thy only friend--'twas then Thou sought'st the arms of Princess Eboli--

A demon's arms! 'Twas she betrayed thee, Carlos! I saw thee fly to her--a dire foreboding Struck on my heart--I followed thee too late! Already wert thou prostrate at her feet, The dread avowal had escaped thy lips-- No way was left to save thee.

CARLOS.

No! her heart Was moved, thou dost mistake, her heart was moved.

MARQUIS.

Night overspread my mind. No remedy, No refuge, no retreat was left to me In nature's boundless compass. Blind despair Transformed me to a fury--to a tiger-- I raised my dagger to a woman's breast. But in that moment--in that dreadful moment-- A radiant sunbeam fell upon my soul.

"Could I mislead the king! Could I succeed In making him think me the criminal! However improbable, the very guilt Will be enough to win the king's belief. I'll dare the task--a sudden thunderbolt May make the tyrant start--what want I further? He stops to think, and Carlos thus gains time To fly to Brussels."

CARLOS.

And hast thou done this?

MARQUIS.

I have despatched a letter to Prince William, Saying I loved the queen, and had escaped The king's mistrust in the unjust suspicion Which falsely fell on thee--that I had found Means, through the monarch's favor, to obtain Free access to the queen. I added, further, That I was fearful of discovery-- That thou hadst learned my secret, and hadst sped To Princess Eboli, with hopes through her To warn the queen--that I had made thee prisoner-- And now that all seemed lost, I had resolved To fly to Brussels. This same letter I----

CARLOS

(Interrupts him, terrified). Hast surely not intrusted to the post! Thou knowest that letters to Brabant and Flanders----

MARQUIS.

Are given to the king; and as things go Taxis would seem to have discharged his duty.

CARLOS.

Heavens! then I'm lost.

How lost? What meanest thou?

CARLOS.

And thou, alas! art lost together with me-- This dreadful fraud my father ne'er will pardon.

MARQUIS.

This fraud! Thou'rt mad! Who will disclose it to him?

CARLOS

(Regards him with a fixed look). Who! Dost thou ask? I will myself.

MARQUIS.

Thou ravest! Stand back----

CARLOS.

Away! For heaven's sake hold me not. While I stay here, he's hiring the assassins.

MARQUIS.

Then is our time more precious--and we still Have much to say.

CARLOS.

What! Before all is finished?

[He makes another effort to go. The MARQUIS holds him by the arm, and looks at him impressively.

Carlos! was I so scrupulous--so eager-- When thou, a boy, didst shed thy blood for me?

CARLOS

(With emotion, and full of admiration). Kind Providence!

MARQUIS.

Reserve thyself for Flanders!

The kingdom is thy destiny--'tis mine To give my life for thee.

CARLOS

(takes his hand with deep sensibility). No, no! he will not, Cannot resist a virtue so sublime.

I will conduct thee to him, and together, Arm linked in arm, will we appear before him. Then thus will I address him: "Father, see, This is the way a friend acts towards his friend." Trust me, 'twill move him--it will touch his heart. He's not without humanity,--my father.

Yes, it will move him. With hot tears, his eyes Will overflow--and he will pardon us.

[A shot is fired through the iron grating. CARLOS leaps up. Whom was that meant for?

MARQUIS (sinking down). I believe--for me.

CARLOS (falling to the earth with a loud cry of grief). O God of mercy!

He is quick--the king.

I had hoped--a little longer--Carlos--think

Of means of flight--dost hear me?--of thy flight. Thy mother--knows it all--I can no more.

[Dies. [CARLOS remains by the corpse, like one bereft of life.

After some time the KING enters, accompanied by many GRANDEES; and starts, panic-struck, at the sight. A general and deep silence. The GRANDEES range themselves in a semi-circle round them both, and regard the KING and his SON alternately. The latter continues without any sign of life. The KING regards him in thoughtful silence.

SCENE IV.

The KING, CARLOS, the DUKESS ALVA, FERIA, and MEDINA SIDONIA, PRINCE OF PARMA, COUNT LERMA, DOMINGO, and numerous GRANDEES.

KING (in a gentle tone).

Thy prayer hath met a gracious hearing, prince, And here I come, with all the noble peers Of this my court, to bring thee liberty.

[CARLOS raises his eyes and looks around him like one awakened from a dream. His eyes are fixed now on the KING, now on the corpse; he gives no answer.

Receive thy sword again. We've been too rash!

[He approaches him, holds out his hand, and assists him to rise.

My son's not in his place; Carlos, arise!

Come to thy father's arms! His love awaits thee.

CARLOS (receives the embrace of the KING without any consciousness.

Suddenly recollects himself, pauses and looks fixedly at him). Thou smell'st of blood-- no, I cannot embrace thee! [Pushes his father back. All the GRANDEES are in commotion. CARLOS to them:-- Nay, stand not there confounded and amazed!-- What monstrous action have I done? Defiled The anointed of the Lord! Oh, fear me not,

I would not lay a hand on him. Behold, Stamped on his forehead is the damning brand! The hand of God hath marked him!

KING

(About to go quickly). Nobles! follow.

CARLOS.

Whither? You stir not from this spot.

[Detaining the KING forcibly with both hands, while with one he manages to seize the sword which the KING has brought with him, and it comes from the scabbard.

KING.

What! Draw

A sword upon thy father?

ALL THE GRANDEES (drawing their swords).

Regicide!

CARLOS (holding the KING firmly with one hand, the naked sword in the other).

Put up your swords! What! Think you I am mad? I am not so: or you were much to blame Thus to remind me, that upon the point

Of this my sword, his trembling life doth hover. I pray you, stand aloof; for souls like mine Need soothing. There--hold back! And with the king What I have yet to settle touches not

Your loyalty. See there--his hand is bloody! Do you not see it? And now look you here!

[Pointing to the corpse.

This hath he done with a well-practised hand.

KING (to the GRANDEES, who press anxiously around him). Retire! Why do you tremble? Are we not

Father and son? I will yet wait and see To what atrocious crime his nature----

CARLOS.

Nature I know her not. Murder is now the word! The bonds of all humanity are severed,

Thine own hands have dissolved them through the realm. Shall I respect a tie which thou hast scorned?

Oh, see! see here! the foulest deed of blood That e'er the world beheld. Is there no God That kings, in his creation, work such havoc? Is there no God, I ask? Since mother's wombs Bore children, one alone--and only one--

So guiltlessly hath died. And art thou sensible What thou hast done? Oh, no! he knows it not: Knows not that he has robbed--despoiled the world Of a more noble, precious, dearer life

Than he and all his century can boast.

KING (with a tone of softness).

If I have been too hasty, Carlos—thou For whom I have thus acted, should at least Not call me to account.

CARLOS.

Is't possible!

Did you then never guess how dear to me Was he who here lies dead? Thou lifeless corpse! Instruct him--aid his wisdom, to resolve

This dark enigma now. He was my friend.

195

And would you know why he has perished thus? He gave his life for me.

KING.

Ha? my suspicions!

CARLOS.

Pardon, thou bleeding corpse, that I profane Thy virtue to such ears. But let him blush With deep-felt shame, the crafty politician, That his gray-headed wisdom was o'erreached, E'en by the judgment of a youth. Yes, sire, We two were brothers! Bound by nobler bands Than nature ties. His whole life's bright career Was love. His noble death was love for me.

E'en in the moment when his brief esteem Exalted you, he was my own. And when

With fascinating tongue he sported with Your haughty, giant mind, 'twas your conceit To bridle him; but you became yourself The pliant tool of his exalted plans. That I became a prisoner, my arrest, Was his deep friendship's meditated work. That letter to Prince William was designed To save my life. It was the first deceit

He ever practised. To insure my safety He rushed on death himself, and nobly perished. You lavished on him all your favor; yet For me he died. Your heart, your confidence, You forced upon him. As a toy he held Your sceptre and your power; he cast them from him, And gave his life for me.

[The KING stands motionless, with eyes fixed on the ground; all the GRANDEES regard him with surprise and alarm.

How could it be That you gave credit to this strange deceit? Meanly indeed he valued you, to try By such coarse artifice to win his ends.

You dared to court his friendship, but gave way Before a test so simple. Oh, no! never

For souls like yours was such a being formed. That well he knew himself, when he rejected Your crowns, your gifts, your greatness, and yourself. This fine-toned lyre broke in your iron hand, And you could do no more than murder him.

ALVA (never having taken his eyes from the KING, and observing his emotion with uneasiness, approaches him with apprehension). Keep not this deathlike silence, sire. Look round, And speak at least to us.

CARLOS.

Once you were not Indifferent to him. And deeply once You occupied his thoughts. It might have been His lot to make you happy. His full heart Might have enriched you; with its mere abundance An atom of his soul had been enough To make a god of you. You've robbed yourself-- Plundered yourself and me. What could you give, To raise again a spirit like to this?

[Deep silence. Many of the GRANDEES turn away, or conceal their faces in their mantles.

Oh, ye who stand around with terror dumb, And mute surprise, do not condemn the youth Who holds this language to the king, his father. Look on this corpse. Behold! for me he died. If ye have tears--if in your veins flow blood, Not molten brass, look here, and blame me not.

[He turns to the KING with more self-possession and calmness. Doubtless you wait the end of this rude scene?

Here is my sword, for you are still my king.

Think not I fear your vengeance. Murder me, As you have murdered this most noble man. My life is forfeit; that I know full well.

But what is life to me? I here renounce All that this world can offer to my hopes. Seek among strangers for a son. Here lies My kingdom.

[He sinks down on the corpse, and takes no part in what follows. A confused tumult and the noise of a crowd is heard in the distance. All is deep silence round the KING. His eyes scan the circle over, but no one returns his looks.

KING.

What! Will no one make reply?

Each eye upon the ground, each look abashed! My sentence is pronounced. I read it here Proclaimed in all this lifeless, mute demeanor. My vassals have condemned me.

[Silence as before. The tumult grows louder. A murmur is heard among the GRANDEES. They exchange embarrassed looks. COUNT LERMA at length gently touches ALVA.

LERMA.

Here's rebellion!

ALVA (in a low voice). I fear it.

LERMA.

It approaches! They are coming!

SCENE V.

An officer of the Body Guard. The former. OFFICER (urgently).

Rebellion! Where's the king?

[He makes his way through the crowd up to the KING. Madrid's in arms!

To thousands swelled, the soldiery and people Surround the palace; and reports are spread That Carlos is a prisoner--that his life Is threatened. And the mob demand to see Him living, or Madrid will be in flames.

THE GRANDEES (with excitement). Defend the king!

ALVA (to the KING, who remains quiet and unmoved). Fly, sire! your life's in danger.

As yet we know not who has armed the people.

KING

(Rousing from his stupor, and advancing with dignity among then). Stands my throne firm, and am I sovereign yet Over this empire? No! I'm king no more. These cowards weep--moved by a puny boy. They only wait the signal to desert me.

I am betrayed by rebels!

ALVA.

Dreadful thought!

KING.

There! fling yourselves before him--down before The young, the expectant king; I'm nothing now But a forsaken, old, defenceless man!

ALVA.

Spaniards! is't come to this?

[All crowd round the KING, and fall on their knees before him with drawn swords. CARLOS remains alone with the corpse, deserted by all.

KING

(Tearing off his mantle and throwing it from him). There! clothe him now

With this my royal mantle; and on high

Bear him in triumph o'er my trampled corpse!

[He falls senseless in ALVA's and LERMA's arms.

LERMA.

For heaven's sake, help!

FERIA.

Oh, sad, disastrous chance!

LERMA.

He faints!

ALVA (leaves the KING in LERMA's and FERIA's hands). Attend his majesty! whilst I Make it my aim to tranquillize Madrid.

[Exit ALVA. The KING is borne off, attended by all the grandees.

SCENE VI.

CARLOS remains behind with the corpse. After a few moments Louis MERCADO appears, looks cautiously round him, and stands a long time silent behind the PRINCE, who does not observe him.

MERCADO.

I come, prince, from her majesty the queen.

[CARLOS turns away and makes no reply. My name, Mercado, I'm the queen's physician See my credentials.

[Shows the PRINCE a signet ring. CARLOS remains still silent.

And the queen desires To speak with you to-day--on weighty business.

CARLOS.

Nothing is weighty in this world to me.

MERCADO.

A charge the Marquis Posa left with her.

CARLOS (looking up quickly). Indeed! I come this instant.

MERCADO.

No, not yet, Most gracious prince! you must delay till night. Each avenue is watched, the guards are doubled You ne'er could reach the palace unperceived; You would endanger everything.

CARLOS.

And yet----

MERCADO.

I know one means alone that can avail us.

'Tis the queen's thought, and she suggests it to you; But it is bold, adventurous, and strange!

CARLOS.

What is it?

MERCADO.

A report has long prevailed That in the secret vaults, beneath the palace, At midnight, shrouded in a monk's attire, The emperor's departed spirit walks.

The people still give credit to the tale, And the guards watch the post with inward terror. Now, if you but determine to assume

This dress, you may pass freely through the guards, Until you reach the chamber of the queen, Which this small key will open. Your attire Will save you from attack. But on the spot, Prince! your decision must be made at once. The requisite apparel and the mask Are ready in your chamber. I must haste And take the queen your answer.

CARLOS.

And the hour?

MERCADO.

It is midnight.

CARLOS.

Then inform her I will come. [Exit MERCADO.

SCENE VII.

CARLOS and COUNT LERMA.

LERMA.

Save yourself, prince! The king's enraged against you. Your liberty, if not your life's in danger!

Ask me no further--I have stolen away To give you warning--fly this very instant!

CARLOS.

Heaven will protect me!

LERMA.

As the queen observed To me, this moment, you must leave Madrid This very day, and fly to Brussels, prince.

Postpone it not, I pray you. The commotion Favors your flight. The queen, with this design, Has raised it. No one will presume so far As to lay hand on you. Swift steeds await you At the Carthusian convent, and behold, Here are your weapons, should you be attacked.
[LERMA gives him a dagger and pistols.

CARLOS.

Thanks, thanks, Count Lerma!

LERMA.

This day's sad event Has moved my inmost soul! No faithful friend Will ever love like him. No patriot breathes But weeps for you. More now I dare not say.

CARLOS.

Count Lerma! he who's gone considered you A man of honor.

LERMA.

Farewell, prince, again!

Success attend you! Happier times will come-- But I shall be no more. Receive my homage!

[Falls on one knee.

CARLOS (endeavors to prevent him, with much emotion). Not so--not so, count! I am too much moved--

I would not be unmanned!

LERMA (kissing his hand with feeling). My children's king!

To die for you will be their privilege!

It is not mine, alas! But in those children Remember me! Return in peace to Spain. May you on Philip's throne feel as a man, For you have learned to suffer! Undertake No bloody deed against your father, prince! Philip compelled his father to yield up The throne to him; and this same Philip now Trembles at his own son. Think, prince, of that And may Heaven prosper and direct your path!

[Exit quickly. CARLOS about to hasten away by another side, but turns rapidly round, and throws himself down before the copse, which he again folds in his arms. He then hurries from the room.

SCENE VIII.

The KING's Antechamber.

DUKE ALVA and DUKE FERIA enter in conversation.

ALVA.

The town is quieted. How is the king?

In the most fearful state. Within his chamber He is shut up, and whatso'er may happen He will admit no person to his presence. The treason of the marquis has at once Changed his whole nature. We no longer know him.

ALVA.

I must go to him, nor respect his feelings. A great discovery which I have made----

FERIA.

A new discovery!

ALVA.

A Carthusian monk My guards observed, with stealthy footsteps, creep Into the prince's chamber, and inquire With anxious curiosity, about

The Marquis Posa's death. They seized him straight, And questioned him. Urged by the fear of death, He made confession that he bore about him Papers of high importance, which the marquis Enjoined him to deliver to the prince, If, before sunset, he should not return.

FERIA.

Well, and what further?

ALVA.

These same letters state That Carlos from Madrid must fly before The morning dawn.

FERIA.

Indeed!

ALVA.

And that a ship at Cadiz lies Ready for sea, to carry him to Flushing.

And that the Netherlands but wait his presence, To shake the Spanish fetters from their arms.

FERIA.

Can this be true?

ALVA.

And other letters say A fleet of Soliman's will sail for Rhodes, According to the treaty, to attack The Spanish squadron in the Midland seas.

FERIA.

Impossible.

ALVA.

And hence I understand The object of the journeys, which of late

The marquis made through Europe. 'Twas no less Than to rouse all the northern powers to arms In aid of Flanders' freedom.

FERIA.

Was it so?

ALVA.

There is besides appended to these letters The full concerted plan of all the war Which is to disunite from Spain's control The Netherlands forever. Naught omitted; The power and opposition close compared; All the resources accurately noted, Together with the maxims to be followed, And all the treaties which they should conclude. The plan is fiendish, but 'tis no less splendid.

FERIA.

The deep, designing traitor!

ALVA.

And, moreover, There is allusion made, in these same letters, To some mysterious conference the prince Must with his mother hold upon the eve Preceding his departure.

FERIA.

That must be This very day.

ALVA.

At midnight. But for this I have already taken proper steps.

You see the case is pressing. Not a moment Is to be lost. Open the monarch's chamber.

FERIA.

Impossible! All entrance is forbidden.

ALVA.

I'll open then myself; the increasing danger Must justify my boldness.

[As he is on the point of approaching the door it opens, and the KING comes out.

FERIA.

'Tis himself.

SCENE IX.

The KING. The preceding.

All are alarmed at his appearance, fall back, and let him pass through them. He appears to be in a waking dream, like a sleep-walker. His dress and figure indicate the disorder caused by his late fainting. With slow steps he walks past the GRANDEES and looks at each with a fixed eye, but without recognizing any of them. At last he stands still, wrapped in thought, his eyes fixed on the ground, till the emotions of his mind gradually express themselves in words.

KING.

Restore me back the dead! Yes, I must have him.

DOMINGO (whispering to ALVA). Speak to him, duke.

KING.

He died despising me!

Have him again I must, and make him think More nobly of me.

ALVA (approaching with fear).

Sire!

KING (looking round the circle). Who speaks to me!

Have you forgotten who I am? Why not Upon your knees, before your king, ye creatures! Am I not still your king? I must command Submission from you. Do you all then slight me Because one man despised me?

ALVA.

Gracious king!

No more of him: a new and mightier foe Arises in the bosom of your realm.

FERIA.

Prince Carlos----

KING.

Had a friend who died for him;

For him! With me he might have shared an empire. How he looked down upon me! From the throne Kings look not down so proudly. It was plain How vain his conquest made him. His keen sorrow Confessed how great his loss. Man weeps not so For aught that's perishable. Oh, that he might

But live again! I'd give my Indies for it! Omnipotence! thou bring'st no comfort to me: Thou canst not stretch thine arm into the grave To rectify one little act, committed With hasty rashness, 'gainst the life of man. The dead return no more. Who dare affirm That I am happy? In the tomb he dwells,

Who scorned to flatter me. What care I now For all who live? One spirit, one free being, And one alone, arose in all this age!

He died despising me!

ALVA.

Our lives are useless!

Spaniards, let's die at once! E'en in the grave This man still robs us of our monarch's heart. KING (sits down, and leans his head on his arm). Oh! had he died for me! I loved him, too, And much. Dear to me was he as a son.

In his young mind there brightly rose for me A new and beauteous morning. Who can say What I had destined for him? He to me Was a first love. All Europe may condemn me, Europe may overwhelm me with its curse,

But I deserved his thanks.

DOMINGO.

What spell is this?

KING.

And, say, for whom did he desert me thus? A boy,--my son? Oh, no, believe it not!

A Posa would not perish for a boy; The scanty flame of friendship could not fill A Posa's heart. It beat for human kind.

His passion was the world, and the whole course Of future generations yet unborn.

To do them service he secured a throne-- And lost it. Such high treason 'gainst mankind Could Posa e'er forgive himself? Oh, no; I know his feelings better. Not that he Carlos preferred to Philip, but the youth-- The tender pupil,--to the aged monarch.

The father's evening sunbeam could not ripen His novel projects. He reserved for this The young son's orient rays. Oh, 'tis undoubted, They wait for my decease.

ALVA.

And of your thoughts, Read in these letters strongest confirmation.

KING.

'Tis possible he may miscalculate.

I'm still myself. Thanks, Nature, for thy gifts; I feel within my frame the strength of youth; I'll turn their schemes to mockery. His virtue Shall be an empty dream--his death, a fool's. His fall shall crush his friend and age together.

We'll test it now--how they can do without me. The world is still for one short evening mine, And this same evening will I so employ, That no reformer yet to cone shall reap Another harvest, in the waste I'll leave, For ten long generations after me.

He would have offered me a sacrifice To his new deity--humanity!

So on humanity I'll take revenge.

And with his puppet I'll at once commence.

[To the DUKE ALVA.

What you have now to tell me of the prince, Repeat. What tidings do these letters bring?

These letters, sire, contain the last bequest Of Posa to Prince Carlos.

KING (reads the papers, watched by all present. He then lays them aside and walks in silence up and down the room).

Summon straight The cardinal inquisitor; and beg He will bestow an hour upon the king, This very night!

TAXIS.

Just on the stroke of two The horses must be ready and prepared, At the Carthusian monastery.

ALVA.

Spies Despatched by me, moreover, have observed Equipments at the convent for a journey, On which the prince's arms were recognized.

FERIA.

And it is rumored that large sums are raised In the queen's name, among the Moorish agents, Destined for Brussels.

KING.

Where is Carlos?

ALVA.

With Posa's body.

KING.

And there are lights as yet Within the queen's apartments?

ALVA.

Everything Is silent there. She has dismissed her maids Far earlier than as yet has been her custom. The Duchess of Arcos, who was last with her, Left her in soundest sleep.

[An officer of the Body Guard enters, takes the DUKE OF FERIA aside, and whispers to him. The latter, struck with surprise, turns to DUKE ALVA. The others crowd round him, and a murmuring noise arises.

FERIA, TAXIS, and DOMINGO (at the same time) 'Tis wonderful!

KING.

What is the matter!

FERIA.

News scarce credible!

DOMINGO.

Two soldiers, who have just returned from duty, Report--but--oh, the tale's ridiculous!

KING.

What do they say?

ALVA.

They say, in the left wing Of the queen's palace, that the emperor's ghost Appeared before them, and with solemn gait Passed on. This rumor is confirmed by all

The sentinels, who through the whole pavilion Their watches keep. And they, moreover, add, The phantom in the queen's apartment vanished.

KING.

And in what shape appeared it?

OFFICER.

In the robes, The same attire he in Saint Justi wore For the last time, apparelled as a monk.

KING.

A monk! And did the sentries know his person Whilst he was yet alive? They could not else Determine that it was the emperor.

OFFICER.

The sceptre which he bore was evidence It was the emperor.

DOMINGO.

And the story goes He often has been seen in this same dress.

Did no one speak to him?

OFFICER.

No person dared.

The sentries prayed, and let him pass in silence.

KING.

The phantom vanished in the queen's apartments!

OFFICER.

In the queen's antechamber. [General silence.

KING (turns quickly round). What say you?

ALVA.

Sire! we are silent.

KING

(After some thought, to the OFFICER). Let my guards be ready

And under arms, and order all approach To that wing of the palace to be stopped.

I fain would have a word with this same ghost. [Exit OFFICER. Enter a PAGE.

PAGE.

The cardinal inquisitor. KING (to all present).

Retire!

[The CARDINAL INQUISITOR, an old man of ninety, and blind, enters, supported on a staff, and led by two Dominicans. The GRANDEES fall on their knees as he passes, and touch the hem of his garment. He gives them his blessing, and they depart.

SCENE X.

The KING and the GRAND INQUISITOR. A long silence.

GRAND INQUISITOR.

Say, do I stand before the king?

KING.

You do.

GRAND INQUISITOR.

I never thought it would be so again!

KING.

I now renew the scenes of early youth,

When Philip sought his sage instructor's counsel.

GRAND INQUISITOR.

Your glorious sire, my pupil, Charles the Fifth, Nor sought or needed counsel at my hands.

KING.

So much happier he! I, cardinal, Am guilty of a murder, and no rest----

GRAND INQUISITOR.

What was the reason for this murder?

KING.

'Twas A fraud unparalleled----

GRAND INQUISITOR.

I know it all.

KING.

What do you know? Through whom, and since what time?

GRAND INQUISITOR.

For years--what you have only learned since sunset. KING (with astonishment).

You know this man then!

GRAND INQUISITOR.

All his life is noted

From its commencement to its sudden close, In Santa Casa's holy registers.

KING.

Yet he enjoyed his liberty!

GRAND INQUISITOR.

The chain With which he struggled, but which held him bound, Though long, was firm, nor easy to be severed.

KING.

He has already been beyond the kingdom.

GRAND INQUISITOR.

Where'er he travelled I was at his side.

KING (walks backwards and forwards in displeasure). You knew the hands, then, I had fallen into; And yet delayed to warn me!

GRAND INQUISITOR.

This rebuke I pay you back. Why did you not consult us Before you sought the arms of such a man?

You knew him: one sole glance unmasked him to you. Why did you rob the office of its victim?

Are we thus trifled with! When majesty Can stoop to such concealment, and in secret, Behind our backs, league with our enemies, What must our fate be then? If one be spared What plea can justify the fate of thousands?

KING.

But he, no less, has fallen a sacrifice.

GRAND INQUISITOR.

No; he is murdered--basely, foully murdered. The blood that should so gloriously have flowed To honor us has stained the assassin's hand.

What claim had you to touch our sacred rights? He but existed, by our hands to perish.

God gave him to this age's exigence, To perish, as a terrible example, And turn high-vaunting reason into shame. Such was my long-laid plan--behold, destroyed In one brief hour, the toil of many years.

We are defrauded, and your only gain Is bloody hands.

Passion impelled me to it. Forgive me.

GRAND INQUISITOR.

Passion! And does royal Philip Thus answer me? Have I alone grown old?

[Shaking his head angrily.

Passion! Make conscience free within your realms, If you're a slave yourself.

KING.

In things like this I'm but a novice. Bear in patience with me.

GRAND INQUISITOR.

No, I'm ill pleased with you--to see you thus Tarnish the bygone glories of your reign.

Where is that Philip, whose unchanging soul, Fixed as the polar star in heaven above, Round its own axis still pursued its course?

Is all the memory of preceding years Forever gone? And did the world become New moulded when you stretched your hand to him?

Was poison no more poison? Did distinction 'Twixt good and evil, truth and falsehood, vanish? What then is resolution? What is firmness?

What is the faith of man, if in one weak, Unguarded hour, the rules of threescore years Dissolve in air, like woman's fickle favor?

I looked into his eyes. Oh, pardon me This weak relapse into mortality.

The world has one less access to your heart; Your eyes are sunk in night.

GRAND INQUISITOR.

What did this man Want with you? What new thing could he adduce, You did not know before? And are you versed

So ill with fanatics and innovators?

Does the reformer's vaunting language sound So novel to your ears? If the firm edifice Of your conviction totters to mere words, Should you not shudder to subscribe the fate Of many thousand poor, deluded souls Who mount the flaming pile for nothing worse?

KING.

I sought a human being. These Domingos----

GRAND INQUISITOR.

How! human beings! What are they to you? Cyphers to count withal--no more! Alas!

And must I now repeat the elements Of kingly knowledge to my gray-haired pupil? An earthly god must learn to bear the want Of what may be denied him. When you whine For sympathy is not the world your equal?

What rights should you possess above your equals?

KING

(throwing himself into a chair). I'm a mere suffering mortal, that I feel;

And you demand from me, a wretched creature, What the Creator only can perform.

GRAND INQUISITOR.

No, sire; I am not thus to be deceived.

I see you through. You would escape from us. The church's heavy chains pressed hard upon you; You would be free, and claim your independence.

[He pauses. The KING is silent.

We are avenged. Be thankful to the church, That checks you with the kindness of a mother. The erring choice you were allowed to make Has proved your punishment. You stand reproved! Now you may turn to us again. And know

If I, this day, had not been summoned here, By Heaven above! before to-morrow's sun, You would yourself have stood at my tribunal!

KING.

Forbear this language, priest. Restrain thyself. I'll not endure it from thee. In such tones

No tongue shall speak to me.

GRAND INQUISITOR.

Then why, O king Call up the ghost of Samuel? I've anointed Two monarchs to the throne of Spain. I hoped To leave behind a firm-established work.

I see the fruit of all my life is lost.

Don Philip's hands have shattered what I built.

But tell me, sire, wherefore have I been summoned? What do I hear? I am not minded, king, To seek such interviews again.

KING.

But one One service more--the last--and then in peace Depart. Let all the past be now forgotten--

Let peace be made between us. We are friends.

GRAND INQUISITOR.

When Philip bends with due humility.

KING

(After a pause).

My son is meditating treason.

GRAND INQUISITOR,

Well!

And what do you resolve?

KING.

On all, or nothing.

GRAND INQUISITOR.

What mean you by this all?

KING.

He must escape, Or die.

GRAND INQUISITOR.

Well, sire! decide.

KING.

And can you not Establish some new creed to justify The bloody murder of one's only son?

GRAND INQUISITOR.

To appease eternal justice God's own Son Expired upon the cross.

KING.

And can you spread This creed throughout all Europe?

GRAND INQUISITOR.

Ay, as far As the true cross is worshipped.

KING.

But I sin-- Sin against nature. Canst thou, by thy power, Silence her mighty voice.

GRAND INQUISITOR.

The voice of nature Avails not over faith.

KING.

My right to judge I place within your hands. Can I retrace The step once taken?

GRAND INQUISITOR.

Give him to me!

KING.

My only son! For whom then have I labored?

GRAND INQUISITOR.

For the grave rather than for liberty!

KING (rising up).

We are agreed. Come with me.

GRAND INQUISITOR.

Monarch! Whither

KING.

From his own father's hands to take the victim. [Leads him away.

SCENE XI.

Queen's Apartment.

CARLOS. The QUEEN. Afterwards the KING and attendants. CARLOS in monk's attire, a mask over his face, which he is just taking off; under his arm a naked sword. It is quite dark. He approaches a door, which is in the act of opening. The QUEEN comes out in her night-dress with a lighted candle. CARLOS falls on one knee before her.

CARLOS.

Elizabeth!

QUEEN (regarding him with silent sorrow). Do we thus meet again?

CARLOS.

'Tis thus we meet again! [A silence.

QUEEN (endeavoring to collect herself).

Carlos, arise!

We must not now unnerve each other thus. The mighty dead will not be honored now By fruitless tears. Tears are for petty sorrows! He gave himself for thee! With his dear life He purchased thine. And shall this precious blood Flow for a mere delusion of the brain?

Oh, Carlos, I have pledged myself for thee. On that assurance did he flee from hence More satisfied. Oh, do not falsify

My word.

CARLOS (with animation) To him I'll raise a monument Nobler than ever honored proudest monarch, And o'er his dust a paradise shall bloom!

QUEEN.

Thus did I hope to find thee! This was still The mighty purpose of his death. On me Devolves the last fulfilment of his plans, And I will now fulfil my solemn oath.

Yet one more legacy your dying friend Bequeathed to me. I pledged my word to him, And wherefore should I now conceal it from you? To me did he resign his Carlos—I Defy suspicion, and no longer tremble Before mankind, but will for once assume

The courage of a friend; My heart shall speak. He called our passion--virtue! I believe him, And will my heart no longer----

CARLOS.

Hold, O queen!

Long was I sunk in a delusive dream. I loved, but now I am at last awake Forgotten be the past. Here are your letters,-- Destroy my own. Fear nothing from my passion, It is extinct. A brighter flame now burns,

And purifies my being. All my love Lies buried in the grave. No mortal wish Finds place within this bosom.

[After a pause, taking her hand. I have come To bid farewell to you, and I have learned

There is a higher, greater good, my mother, Than to call thee mine own. One rapid night Has winged the tardy progress of my years, And prematurely ripened me to manhood.

I have no further business in the world, But to remember him. My harvest now Is ended.

[He approaches the QUEEN, who conceals her face. Mother! will you not reply!

QUEEN.

Carlos! regard not these my tears. I cannot Restrain then. But believe me I admire you.

CARLOS.

Thou wert the only partner of our league And by this name thou shalt remain to me The most beloved object in this world.

No other woman can my friendship share, More than she yesterday could win my love. But sacred shall the royal widow be, Should Providence conduct me to the throne.

[The KING, accompanied by the GRAND INQUISITOR, appears in the background without being observed.

I hasten to leave Spain, and never more Shall I behold my father in this world. No more I love him. Nature is extinct Within this breast. Be you again his wife-- His son's forever lost to him! Return Back to your course of duty--I must speed To liberate a people long oppressed

From a fell tyrant's hand. Madrid shall hail Carlos as king, or ne'er behold him more. And now a long and last farewell---- [He kisses her.

QUEEN.

Oh, Carlos!

How you exalt me! but I dare not soar To such a height of greatness:--yet I may Contemplate now your noble mind with wonder.

CARLOS.

Am I not firm, Elizabeth? I hold thee Thus in my arms and tremble not. The fear Of instant death had, yesterday, not torn me From this dear spot. [He leaves her.

All that is over now, And I defy my mortal destinies.

I've held thee in these arms and wavered not. Hark! Heard you nothing!

[A clock strikes.

QUEEN.

Nothing but the bell That tolls the moment of our separation.

CARLOS.

Good night, then, mother! And you shall, from Ghent, Receive a letter, which will first proclaim Our secret enterprise aloud. I go To dare King Philip to an open contest.

Henceforth there shall be naught concealed between us! You need not shun the aspect of the world.

Be this my last deceit.

[About to take up the mask--the KING stands between them.

KING.

It is thy last.

[The QUEEN falls senseless.

CARLOS (hastens to her and supports her in his arms). Is the queen dead? Great heavens!

KING (coolly and quietly to the GRAND INQUISITOR).

Lord Cardinal!

I've done my part. Go now, and do your own.

[Exit.

CONTENIDO

Don Carlos A Play	1
Frederich Schiller	**Error! Bookmark not defined.**
ACT I.	2
SCENE I.	2
SCENE II.	6
SCENE III.	13
SCENE IV.	17
SCENE V.	22
SCENE VI.	29
SCENE VII.	32
SCENE IX.	34
ACT II.	37
SCENE I.	37
SCENE II.	39
SCENE III.	45
SCENE IV.	47
SCENE V.	50
SCENE VI.	54
SCENE VIII.	57
SCENE IX.	68
SCENE X.	70
SCENE XI.	74
SCENE XII.	77
SCENE XIII.	80
SCENE XIV.	81
SCENE XV.	83
ACT III.	90
SCENE I.	90
SCENE II.	91
SCENE III.	94
SCENE IV.	98
SCENE V.	102
SCENE VI.	103

SCENE VII.	104
SCENE VIII.	107
SCENE IX.	108
SCENE X.	109
ACT IV.	119
SCENE I.	119
SCENE II.	121
SCENE III.	122
SCENE IV.	128
SCENE V.	132
SCENE VI.	137
SCENE VII.	138
SCENE VIII.	139
SCENE IX.	140
SCENE X.	146
SCENE XI.	147
SCENE XII.	148
SCENE XIII.	152
SCENE XIV.	156
SCENE XV.	159
SCENE XVI.	161
SCENE XVII.	162
SCENE XVIII.	163
SCENE XIX.	164
SCENE XX.	168
SCENE XXI.	169
SCENE XXII.	175
SCENE XXIII.	179
SCENE XXIV.	182
ACT V.	184
SCENE I.	184
SCENE II.	187
SCENE III.	189
SCENE IV.	194

SCENE V. 198
SCENE VI. 200
SCENE VII. 202
SCENE VIII. 204
SCENE IX. 207
SCENE X. 212
SCENE XI. 218

Printed in Great Britain
by Amazon